I0622861

MASTERING EMOTIONAL INTELLIGENCE WITH EASE

7 STEP GUIDE TO ELEVATE YOUR PERSONAL GROWTH BY IMPROVING SELF-AWARENESS, BUILDING EMOTIONAL RESILIENCE, AND ENHANCING YOUR SOCIAL SKILLS

AMBER PRESTON

CONTENTS

INTRODUCTION

Imagine a tornado tearing through a quiet town, uprooting trees, destroying homes, and causing utter chaos in its path. It's wild, unpredictable, and leaves a trail of devastation. Now, imagine that tornado within you—a maelstrom of emotions, whirling and colliding, each gust stronger than the last, leaving you feeling lost and overwhelmed. That, my friend, is the storm of our emotions without the compass of emotional intelligence.

Have you ever wondered why some days you feel utterly crushed by even the smallest hiccup, while on others you can navigate life's challenges with grace and ease? Or how one comment can cause a heated argument, while another day, the same comment rolls off like water off a duck's back?

If so, it's not just you. This book is for the countless souls who've felt the same way: the feeling that emotions rule their days, the constant struggle to understand others, and the yearning for deeper, more meaningful relationships. You didn't pick up this book by chance. Something prompted you, a catalyst. Perhaps it was a failed relationship, a challenging workplace environment, or simply a burning desire to know yourself better.

Now, imagine a world where you can

- truly understand the intricacies of your own emotions and those of others.
- navigate social situations with grace, ease, and genuine connection.
- bounce back from setbacks with renewed vigor and strength.
- engage in enriching and fulfilling relationships.

Doesn't that sound like a dream?

It's no surprise that icons like Oprah Winfrey and Elon Musk credit their success, in part, to their high emotional intelligence. Their ability to connect, understand, and motivate not just themselves but also those around them sets them apart in a world brimming with talent.

By the time you turn the last page, you'll have uncovered

- the underlying principles of emotional intelligence and their profound impact.
- strategies to enhance your self-awareness.
- the pillars of emotional resilience.
- techniques to foster effective communication and social skills.

- insights into cultivating empathy.
- the art of managing relationships for a harmonious life.
- the transformative professional implications of emotional intelligence.

Before these insights were available, many wandered in the dark, grappling with relationships and self-worth, unable to harness the full potential of their emotions. Now, armed with the knowledge in this book, you are set to embark on a transformative journey.

You might wonder why you should heed the guidance within these pages. This book is the culmination of extensive research, real-life experiences, and insights from experts in the field of psychology and emotional intelligence. It's not just a compilation of theories; it's a testament to the countless individuals who've transformed their lives by harnessing the power of their emotions.

Let's be honest; the internet is flooded with information. You could spend hours, days, or even years sifting through articles, attending seminars, and joining workshops. But here, you're presented with a distilled version, a roadmap, cutting through the noise and pointing you toward the core of what truly matters.

Recall the most profound moments in your life. Can you see the thread of emotion weaving through them? The euphoria of achievements, the heartbreak of lost love, the comfort of a friend's embrace, the sting of harsh words. Our lives are colored by our emotions, and this book will help you to develop strategies to be the best, most emotionally intelligent version of yourself.

So, let's journey together through the landscapes of our emotions and discover the harmony that awaits. With every chapter, with every page, you'll move closer to a life where emotions are not a tumultuous storm but a gentle guiding breeze. Welcome to your new beginning.

1

STEP #1—UNDERSTANDING EMOTIONAL INTELLIGENCE

> *There is no separation of mind and emotions; emotions, thinking, and learning are all linked.*

— ERIC JENSEN

Isn't it fascinating how intertwined our thoughts and feelings truly are? Eric Jensen's words echo a truth we've all felt but might not have put into words. We've all had those moments when a sudden emotion shifts our entire perspective or when a deep thought tugs at our heartstrings. This dance between what we feel and think is the essence of emotional intelligence.

Emotional intelligence is not just a buzzword. It's a transformative skill set, a paradigm shift that touches every facet of our lives. From professional advancements to personal well-being, its ripple effect is profound. Cultivating emotional intelligence is akin to investing in oneself, promising a brighter, more fulfilling, and harmonious future.

So, what's the big deal about emotional intelligence? Why not just stick to the good old IQ? Well, let's think of it this way: Imagine navigating through life's ups and downs without truly understanding why we feel the way we do or how those feelings drive our decisions. Sounds challenging, right? That's where this chapter comes in, providing clarity and insight into the world of emotional intelligence.

Ready to dive deep? Let's get started exploring the relationship between our minds and emotions and discovering the true power of emotional intelligence in our lives.

My aim? By the end of this chapter, you won't just have a text-book definition. Instead, you'll have a deep, intuitive understanding that will serve as your compass for the rest of our journey together.

DEFINING EMOTIONAL INTELLIGENCE

Emotional intelligence, often referred to as EQ (Emotional Quotient), is the capacity to recognize, understand, manage, and effectively use emotions in both ourselves and others. This entails not only being aware of our own emotions and those of others but also understanding how those emotions drive behaviors and how to apply this understanding in various situations. In essence, it's about being emotionally aware and using that awareness to navigate our interactions in a thoughtful and effective manner (Cherry, 2023;

Emotional Intelligence Toolkit, n.d.; Mental Health America, n.d.).

Can Everyone Have Emotional Intelligence?

A common concern is whether emotional intelligence is an innate trait or something that can be developed. Here's the reassuring news: While it's been found that only about 36% of individuals can accurately identify their emotions as they happen (*Are You Emotionally Intelligent?*, n.d.), this doesn't mean that the rest lack the capacity for emotional intelligence.

Not everyone might start with high emotional intelligence skills right out of the gate, but everyone possesses the potential to hone and develop these strengths. Just like many abilities in life, building one's EQ isn't necessarily about being born with it but about consistent practice, awareness, and effort. So, if you're concerned about not having a natural aptitude for EQ, remember that emotional intelligence can be cultivated and enhanced with dedication and intention (Schwantes, 2021).

Emotional intelligence stands as a beacon in the realm of personal development and workplace efficiency. With an array of benefits to its name, let's delve deeper into each one to better understand its profound impact.

Reduces Stress

In both personal and professional life, emotional intelligence serves as a shield against the pressures and stresses of the day. Recognizing and managing stress early can lead to a more balanced approach to life's challenges, ultimately improving your physical health as well. Reduced stress promotes longevity and boosts energy and motivation, which is beneficial both at home and at work. Furthermore, lower stress levels can improve family relationships and make social interactions more enjoyable. On the job, less stress means better focus, increased productivity, and a healthier work-life balance. Less stress in your personal life can even make you a more patient and understanding colleague, forming a virtuous cycle.

Improves Communication Skills

Effective communication is vital both in personal relationships and the workplace. Emotional intelligence helps in reading non-verbal cues and actively listening, thus reducing misunderstandings and fostering fruitful interactions. It also improves your intrapersonal communication, allowing you to operate from a place of self-belief and confidence. Enhanced communication can lead to stronger relationships with friends and family, and it can also boost your performance in team settings at work. Clear communication also means fewer conflicts, which can make your personal and professional life more harmonious. Furthermore, a positive internal dialogue reinforces self-confidence, making challenges easier to face in any environment.

Enhances Social Skills

Social skills are not just for team meetings or casual get-togethers; they are essential for quality interactions in every area of life. High emotional intelligence provides the tools for understanding social scenarios, facilitating effective team collaborations, and enhancing interpersonal relationships. Such skills make you approachable in any setting and a consensus builder in the professional world. In personal life, these skills can deepen friendships and familial relationships by improving mutual understanding and empathy. In the professional setting, individuals with better social skills often find it easier to lead teams and manage projects effectively. Moreover, understanding social cues can help you better navigate complicated social situations both at work and in your personal life.

Creates a Positive Environment

People with high EQ often create nurturing and positive environments, both at home and at work. These atmospheres not only enhance job satisfaction but also make personal relationships more meaningful. In such environments, conflicts are resolved amicably, and the overall morale remains high. A positive environment at home contributes to emotional well-being, which in turn reflects positively at work. Likewise, a harmonious workplace can reduce stress and make your personal life more peaceful. The skills you gain from creating a positive environment at work can also be applied to improve your home life, leading to a more satisfying and integrated life experience.

Specific Benefits to Employees

In today's complex and rapidly evolving workplace, emotional intelligence has emerged as a critical skill for employees aiming for professional excellence. Beyond the standard metrics of performance and technical expertise, EQ offers an added layer of capabilities that can be the distinguishing factor in career advancement, team collaboration, and overall job satisfaction. As we navigate through the intricacies of modern corporate dynamics, understanding the specific benefits of emotional intelligence becomes pivotal for both individual contributors and leaders. Here, we delve into how a well-developed EQ can significantly enhance various aspects of an employee's professional life while also enriching their personal experiences.

Helps Employees to Move to the Next Level

Emotional intelligence is not just about recognizing emotions but leveraging them for career advancement. It aids in self-awareness and self-management, helping employees make informed decisions and maintain composure in high-pressure situations. These skills pave the way for professional growth and leadership roles while also improving personal decision-making capabilities. By being more self-aware, you can identify the skills you need to improve, which can be useful in both your career and personal development plans. Good self-management skills can help you navigate personal challenges more effectively, from finances to relationships. These universally useful skills make emotional intelligence indispensable for holistic growth.

Teaches Employees How to React to Constructive Criticism

In the professional world, constructive criticism is a path to growth. High EQ means you perceive this feedback as an opportunity for improvement rather than a personal attack. This constructive mindset aids in professional development and personal growth, as you can apply the feedback to improve both work-related skills and personal habits. Learning to accept and utilize feedback in a work setting can translate into being more open to constructive comments in your personal relationships, thus fostering growth in both areas. Furthermore, this skill makes you more adaptable and agile, both as a professional and an individual, enabling you to face life's unpredictability with resilience.

Helps Employees Conquer Their Fears, Doubts, and Insecurities

Understanding and overcoming emotional barriers can aid in personal and professional development. By addressing the root causes of these fears, employees build greater self-confidence and dismantle limiting beliefs. This enhanced self-concept encourages them to take calculated risks, accept new challenges, and actualize their full potential both at work and in personal endeavors. Overcoming fears and insecurities can open the doors to new opportunities, be it a promotion at work or taking the leap into a new hobby or relationship. Moreover, the confidence gained through overcoming fears can make you a role model, inspiring both colleagues and loved ones to challenge their own limitations. The ability to strategize and confront fears is a universally applicable skill that will serve you well in all walks of life.

The Components of Emotional Intelligence

Emotional intelligence is a multidimensional competency comprising five core components: self-awareness, self-regulation, empathy, motivation, and social skills. While distinct, these facets work synergistically to endow individuals with the tools to excel across personal and professional domains. By developing each area, people can unlock their fullest potential and bring more wisdom, compassion, and success into their lives and organizations. This section will explore the key elements constituting emotional intelligence and how enhancing these skills translates into positive outcomes.

Self-Awareness

Self-awareness involves understanding one's own emotions, strengths, weaknesses, values, and goals. It provides the foundation for personal growth and development. By cultivating self-awareness, individuals can identify areas requiring improvement and play to their natural strengths when pursuing opportunities. This introspective capacity allows for ongoing self-evaluation and refinement. Enhancing self-awareness requires setting aside time for regular reflection through journaling, meditation, and open dialogues with trusted mentors. This inward focus gradually reveals blind spots, uncovers growth opportunities, and breeds self-actualization.

Cultivating self-awareness is like turning a spotlight inward. At first, you squint against the glare, unsure what you'll find in the shadows. But over time, your eyes adjust, allowing you to appreciate the intricate details that define you. The journey reveals unexplored passions, lingering fears, and forgotten dreams. You uncover who you were, who you are, and who you hope to become. With this understanding, you gain the power to rewrite limiting narratives, reinforce developing strengths, and chart an authentic path ahead. Self-awareness lights the way.

Self-Regulation

Self-regulation is the ability to manage emotions and impulses. It allows individuals to think before acting, adapt to changing circumstances, and persevere through challenges. Self-regulation promotes level-headedness and composure even in high-pressure situations. Individuals refrain from knee-jerk reactions, maintaining restraint and rationality. This skill empowers people to respond appropriately to feedback, constructive criticism, and trying scenarios. Techniques like deep breathing, TEMP listening, and cognitive reappraisal can be cultivated to enhance self-regulation. With practice, these become healthy default responses to stress.

Mastering self-regulation is akin to learning an instrument. At first, the scales are shaky, the notes discordant. But with routine practice, your dexterity improves. What once seemed impossible becomes fluid, even automatic. Self-regulation follows a similar trajectory—the skills strengthen through use. Tempering emotional reactions takes diligence; you must catch yourself in the heat of the moment. But the more you pause, process, and respond thoughtfully, the more natural it becomes. Your range expands; you play life's chaotic melodies with poise.

Empathy

Empathy means recognizing and understanding others' perspectives, feelings, and needs. It enables compassionate decision-making and conflict resolution. By seeing through the lens of another, individuals can tailor communications and actions to resonate appropriately. Empathy facilitates fruitful collaborations and reductions in misunderstandings. It is a keystone of healthy interpersonal relationships. Empathy can be strengthened by actively listening, asking thoughtful questions, and suspending one's own assumptions and judgments. This fosters mutual understanding and humanizes those around us.

Empathy blossoms when you water the seeds of human connection. Get curious about strangers; ask heartfelt questions. Listen with raw presence as their stories unfold. Suspend judgment as you step into their shoes. See the beauty that dwells beneath their flaws. Recognize the fears, hopes, and dreams that animate us all. Let empathy flourish, even when distrust seems wiser. Its roots run deep when planted in open soil. In time, you'll notice green shoots of understanding change everything they touch.

Motivation

Motivation pertains to one's drive, optimism, and passion. It empowers people to pursue meaningful goals with resilience. Motivation breeds enthusiasm, initiative, and commitment. Individuals high in motivation view obstacles as opportunities for growth. They operate with a solutions-focused mindset and a belief in their abilities. This mental toughness allows them to actualize their visions. Reframing setbacks, celebrating small wins, and nurturing passions are ways to boost motivation over the long term. This instills the grit and tenacity required for personal and professional excellence.

Motivation is the current that energizes our dreams. Some days the flow is weak; you must coax it along through trial and error. Celebrate when a spark catches; let it energize your purpose. On other days, inspiration strikes like lightning, jolting you with possibility. Channel this surge toward your goals. Motivation ebbs and flows, an endless cycle. During the lulls, reflect on how far you've come. When it crests, ride the wave ever forward. Stay centered through the rhythms; let commitment carry you. With patience and care, motivation becomes an unstoppable force.

Social Skills

Social skills allow individuals to communicate clearly, foster relationships, work in teams, and influence others positively. These competencies facilitate the building of rapport and negotiation of complex group dynamics. Social skills empower employees to become collaborative leaders who can provide constructive feedback, mediate conflict, and promote shared objectives. This ability to navigate interpersonal complexity allows organizations to harness diverse talents harmoniously. Social skills can be honed through public speaking training, volunteering, and proactive relationship-building across the company. With practice, socially intelligent behaviors become second nature.

Social skills are honed through practice, like training for a marathon. At first, the interpersonal terrain feels awkward and draining. But little by little, your endurance builds. You learn to pace yourself, listen intently, and project assured warmth. Your confidence grows with accomplished milestones. Before long, you're traversing complex group dynamics with ease. Yet, always hold a beginner's mind; there is nuance still to learn. Maintain humility, curiosity, and care. In relational fitness, the training never ends. But connection makes the journey profound.

The components of emotional intelligence work in concert to endow individuals with critical skills for navigating life's complexities. While innate temperament plays a role, dedicating time and effort toward developing each facet can yield profound rewards. As individuals level up their emotional intelligence, they gain the self-knowledge, discipline, wisdom, drive, and interpersonal awareness to thrive. Both individuals and organizations stand to benefit enormously from promoting multi-tiered emotional intelligence growth. By making it a priority, people can reach their highest potential and collectively elevate their communities.

SELF-ASSESSMENT EXERCISES TO GAUGE YOUR CURRENT EQ

Gauging one's current emotional intelligence allows for targeted growth and improvement. Through mindful self-evaluation, we can identify areas of strength to leverage as well as skills requiring further cultivation. Various reflective exercises provide valuable data points to enhance our self-awareness. While innate temperament differs, dedicating time to assess and develop your EQ skills will undoubtedly expand your capacity over time.

The EQ Balance Assessment

This exercise evaluates how balanced your EQ skills are across different contexts. For one week, track scenarios where you demonstrate self-awareness, self-regulation, empathy, motivation, and social skills on a scale of 1–5 (1 = poor, 5 = excellent). Calculate your average for each EQ component. A balanced score across categories indicates higher overall emotional intelligence. Make this a weekly practice to benchmark progress over time. Comparing assessments during periods of major stress versus calm can also reveal how challenged environments impact your EQ equilibrium. Strive for consistency.

The EQ Blind Spot Analysis

Have a trusted partner who knows you well complete an abbreviated EQ assessment on your behalf. Then, complete the same assessment about yourself and compare scores. Discrepancies reveal potential blind spots—EQ skills you may under or over-estimate. Explore these further through journaling. Ask your partner follow-up questions about situations demonstrating your blind spots to gain deeper insight. Uncover if these align with past feedback you've resisted. Leverage this knowledge to expand self-awareness.

The EQ Stress Response Evaluation

Note your emotional responses, actions, and recovery times when facing stressors for two weeks. Does your EQ remain steady or fluctuate? Can you identify triggers tied to lower EI? Stronger self-regulation and faster rebound times correlate to higher emotional intelligence. Also reflect on any unhealthy coping mechanisms you turn to during stress. Do you isolate, overeat, or self-medicate? Work to replace these with healthy EI-building practices over time.

The EQ Conflict Resolution Analysis

Reflect on recent conflicts—professional and personal. Analyze your EQ skills demonstrated based on how conflicts arose, were addressed, and resolved. Did you remain calm? Empathize? Communicate effectively? Conflicts engaged through high EQ lead to constructive outcomes. Consider your internal self-talk during the conflict. Did you make negative assumptions? Revisit tough scenarios and reimagine more elevated responses. This strengthens EQ for future clashes.

The EQ Social Litmus Test

Ask trusted acquaintances to describe your top interpersonal strengths and weaknesses. Listen without judgment. Do their perceptions align with your self-assessment? Inconsistencies indicate areas of lower social self-awareness. Use feedback to improve social skills. Discuss positive and negative examples they recall that illuminate your social EQ in action. Uncover what responses elevated or escalated situations. Internalize insights.

Regular emotional intelligence check-ins empower us to become the best version of ourselves. However, the key is to approach assessments from a non-judgmental and growth-oriented mindset. View results as impartial data to inform positive change rather than as fixed evaluations of your worth. With consistent practice, you'll notice measurable improvements in self-awareness, self-regulation, empathy, motivation, and social skills. Celebrate progress made; allow insights to deepen your wisdom. Our emotional intelligence is continually evolving—let self-assessments illuminate the path ahead.

The Impact of EQ on Your Life

Emotional intelligence is not just an abstract concept—it profoundly shapes how we show up in all areas of life. By cultivating our EQ, we can unlock a breadth of tangible benefits in our relationships, careers, and personal growth. Understanding these multifaceted impacts provides motivation to continuously develop our emotional skills. This section will explore how optimized emotional intelligence facilitates both external success and inner fulfillment.

Personal Impacts

High emotional intelligence allows us to engage in healthy relationships built on empathy, vulnerability, and trust. Strong intrapersonal skills make us more aware of our needs and emotions. Interpersonal skills enable us to communicate lovingly, manage conflict constructively, and support our loved ones through challenges. We become steadier partners, parents, and friends. On an individual level, EI fosters inner peace, life satisfaction, and the resilience to navigate adversity. We understand our feelings, channel them productively, and fill our lives with meaning. By approaching relationships with authentic care, active listening, and selflessness, we build our circle of trust. Bonds deepen, and we find fulfillment in nurturing people's growth.

Professional Impacts

Emotionally intelligent employees excel in their careers. Intrapersonal skills like self-motivation and time management allow people to accomplish goals independently. Interpersonal aptitudes, including leadership, collaboration, and conflict resolution, facilitate team cohesion and workplace harmony. Together, these enable professional excellence. Emotionally intelligent individuals also cope effectively with job stress, adapt to changes, and act with integrity. Their composure, people skills, and positivity make them magnets for opportunity. Emotionally intelligent people identify their passions and align their career paths accordingly. They become invested employees who handle workplace relationships skillfully. Their ambition is tempered by wisdom and principle.

Impacts on Growth

On a personal growth trajectory, emotional intelligence is indispensable. Self-awareness provides the foundation for identifying areas requiring improvement; self-regulation gives us the discipline to change habits. Empathy develops compassion; motivation drives us forward. Socially, we learn to give and receive feedback productively. By leveraging these competencies, our emotional intelligence expands—unlocking our greatest potential. With higher EI, we have the self-knowledge to set ambitious goals, perseverance to overcome obstacles, and interpersonal awareness to learn from others. Our journey is amplified exponentially. Growth itself fortifies our emotional intelligence, fueling an upward spiral. We extract lessons from each challenge faced and connections made.

In many ways, emotional intelligence is the master key that opens the door to thriving across interwoven aspects of life. While technical skills may propel isolated domains of achievement, EI enables excellence holistically. Progress in one dimension fuels positive change across the board. Ultimately, a high level of emotional intelligence allows us to build healthy, happy lives of purpose and human connection. The journey brings out our best selves—someone wiser, more compassionate, and better equipped to leave a meaningful legacy. By recognizing

EI's profoundly positive impacts, we can chart a course toward sustainable success.

WRAPPING UP

In exploring the foundations of emotional intelligence, we've uncovered how this meta-ability acts as the cornerstone for fulfillment in life and work. Far more than a passing fad, EI represents a paradigm shift—one that illuminates the critical skills we must cultivate to thrive in an increasingly complex world.

In this chapter, we

- defined emotional intelligence and its components.
- discussed the benefits of EI across personal, professional, and growth domains.
- explored assessments to gauge current EI levels.
- recognized EI's profound impacts on relationships, careers, and self-actualization.

Armed with this knowledge, we can begin leveling up our own emotional intelligence. As we've learned, self-awareness represents the first step in this journey. In the next chapter, we'll explore core practices to enhance self-awareness—spotlighting our inner world so we can navigate life's challenges with greater wisdom and grace. Deepening self-knowledge lights the path ahead.

CASE STUDY: SARAH

Imagine Sarah, a manager at a bustling tech firm. She was competent, diligent, and fiercely committed to her job. But even with all these qualities, she sensed an undercurrent of tension rippling through her team. Things were just not clicking. Puzzled and frustrated, she stumbled upon the concept known as emotional intelligence, or EQ, and it was as if the universe itself sent her a guidebook.

Sarah didn't just skim through the concept; she dove deep. She was hungry for transformation, so she started by looking inward—self-awareness. She asked for 360-degree feedback, not just from her higher-ups but from her team members as well. And let me tell you, she was open enough to listen. The feedback wasn't all roses and sunshine, but it offered her the raw, gritty gift of perspective. She now had a roadmap drawn by others, but for her.

Moving on to self-regulation, she started practicing mindfulness. Who among us hasn't shot off an email in a moment of frustration and regretted it minutes later? Sarah became a master of the pause, giving herself the space to choose her reactions rather than being held hostage by them. The impact this had on her team was like a ripple in a pond—calmness started spreading, and stress levels dipped.

Then came the cornerstone of human connection: empathy. Sarah scheduled one-on-one chats with every single team member. Not to critique or strategize, but to listen, to truly hear the stories each person brought to the table. She replaced judgment with curiosity. The result? Her team started to feel seen, maybe for the first time in their professional lives. They felt safe and valued, and that changed the entire vibe of the workspace.

Motivated to build on this momentum, Sarah took a fresh look at her team's goals. She tailored them to play to each individual's strengths and dovetailed them with their unique aspirations. And this wasn't just managerial flair; this was leadership that was emotionally intelligent, leading from the heart and the head. The team wasn't just clocking in hours now; they were engaged, motivated, and fully showing up.

Lastly, the social maestro that she was becoming, Sarah fostered an environment of genuine teamwork and communication. She built in time for team-building exercises that weren't just about falling back and trusting someone to catch you, but about leaning into difficult conversations, navigating conflict, and coming out stronger together.

In less than a year, this embrace of EQ transformed not just Sarah, but her entire team. Productivity surged by 30%, and staff turnover plunged. She earned the accolade of "Most Improved Leader of the Year," but more than that, she earned the trust and respect of her team. She went to bed each night not just tired, but fulfilled.

CASE STUDY: MARK

Mark's deepening understanding of emotional intelligence didn't just stop at identifying his areas for growth; it was as if he had been given a new lens through which to view the world. Previously, his interactions had been filled with hurried judgments and assumptions, a rush to get to the next thing, and a focus on his own immediate reactions. But once he grasped the importance of each component of emotional intelligence, he started slowing down and examining his thoughts and feelings more closely.

His improved self-awareness allowed him to recognize not just his own emotions but also how they influenced his behavior. The chapter explained that self-awareness was the cornerstone of emotional intelligence. Mark began journaling to track his emotions and their triggers, which became an eye-opening experience for him. He could now preempt feelings of irritation or anger and choose a more constructive response.

Self-regulation, his previously identified weak link, gradually began to strengthen as Mark applied different techniques. He used mindfulness exercises to stay present and focused, which had an unexpected but wonderful benefit—his stress levels started to plummet. He could handle disagreements better, not letting them escalate into full-blown conflicts. Even his friends began to notice how much calmer and more composed he had become in stressful situations.

Empathy was another area in which Mark felt he had room to grow. With a renewed perspective, he started putting himself in others' shoes more often. This made him a more compassionate friend and sibling. Now, when someone shared a concern or problem with him, he took the time to really listen and understand their point of view instead of hastily offering advice. This emotional generosity wasn't lost on his loved ones, who found their conversations with Mark to be increasingly meaningful and nourishing.

Motivation was another aspect of emotional intelligence that the chapter emphasized. Although Mark had always been reasonably driven, understanding the emotional aspects of motivation gave him an energy boost. He set personal goals that went beyond the superficial and found that striving for these deeper objectives made the journey more enjoyable.

His enhanced social skills were the cherry on top. Mark found himself better able to read the room, so to speak, and adapt his behavior accordingly. Whether he was at a casual gathering or a family dinner, he could sense the emotional currents and navigate them more adeptly.

And so, the cycle continued. The more Mark invested in his emotional intelligence, the richer his life became. His relationships thrived, his mental state stabilized, and his overall sense of well-being soared. He had tapped into a kind of emotional eloquence that allowed him to express himself fully and connect with others on a deeper level.

Mark's journey isn't unique; it's a journey open to anyone willing to delve into understanding and enhancing their emotional intelligence. The first step, as Mark discovered, is awareness, and from that foundation, an entirely new way of living and relating to others can flourish. Mark is a living testament to the untapped potential within us all, waiting just beneath the surface, ready to enrich our lives in ways we can't even imagine.

2

STEP #2—DEVELOPING SELF AWARENESS

> *We are dangerous when we are not conscious of our responsibility for how we behave, think, and feel.*

— MARSHALL B. ROSENBERG

It's a powerful thought, isn't it? Rosenberg's words highlight a simple truth: When we're out of touch with our own emotions and motivations, things can quickly go awry. Think about it. How many times have misunderstandings or mistakes happened because we weren't fully tuned into our own feelings or those of others?

This chapter will break down the ins and outs of self-awareness. You'll learn why it's so vital, especially as a foundation of emotional intelligence. And by the time you finish this section, you won't just know what self-awareness is; you'll have tangible ways to grow and maintain it in your everyday life.

WHAT IS SELF-AWARENESS?

At its core, self-awareness is the conscious knowledge and understanding of one's own character, emotions, desires, and motivations. It's the process of reflecting on oneself, understanding personal strengths, weaknesses, and the impact one's actions can have on others. It involves both internal self-awareness—recognizing our own values, passions, and reactions—and external self-awareness—understanding how others perceive us. In essence, it's the ability to see ourselves clearly and objectively through introspection and reflection (Betz, 2022)

How Self-Awareness Helps With Emotional Intelligence

Self-awareness acts as the foundational pillar of emotional intelligence. It's the ability to understand your emotions, recognize their origins, and see their impact on your work and relationships. With solid self-awareness, individuals can more effectively harness their emotions, guiding them in productive directions rather than being controlled by them. By understanding oneself, it becomes easier to empathize with others, communicate effectively, and manage complex social situations. It's the starting point, and from there, other aspects of emotional intelligence—like self-regulation, motivation, and social skills—can be built upon and refined. Essentially, without a keen sense of self-awareness, true emotional intelligence is out of reach (Eurich, 2008).

Benefits of Being Self-Aware

Understanding oneself goes beyond introspection—it's about making active, informed changes in our lives. It's the lens through which we view our actions, reactions, and interactions. From the decisions we make in solitude to the choices we make amidst a crowd, self-awareness is pivotal. So, let's take a closer look at how self-awareness can reframe and redefine our experiences.

Better Management and Regulation of Emotions

When we're deeply in tune with our emotional world, it becomes second nature to manage and modulate our reactions. This doesn't mean suppressing emotions, but rather understanding them to channel them effectively. Such proactive emotional management can result in fewer moments of regret, lessened anxiety, and an overall feeling of control in life's unpredictable tide.

Improved Communication

Clear, concise communication starts with understanding oneself. When we know where we stand, it's easier to stand firm in conversations and to extend a hand in understanding. The ripple effects of this can be seen in daily interactions, leading to fewer conflicts, clearer expressions, and an overall smoother flow of thoughts and feelings.

Enhanced Decision-Making Skills

Decisions grounded in self-awareness are often those we look back on with confidence. We move forward not with uncertainty, but with a clarity that comes from a deep understanding of ourselves. It's this internal compass, shaped by self-awareness, that guides us through the fog of choices, helping us navigate with assurance.

Strengthened Relationships

The beauty of self-awareness is that while it starts with the self, it benefits everyone around us. Understanding oneself sets the stage for understanding others, leading to deeper, more meaningful connections. It's like building a bridge; the stronger the foundation, the more resilient and enduring the structure.

Higher Levels of Happiness

There's a unique contentment that comes from living a life aligned with our core beliefs. Each day feels less like going through the motions and more like a genuine expression of oneself. Over time, this continuous alignment paves the way for a lasting, deep-seated happiness that isn't easily shaken by external factors.

Increased Confidence

Confidence, in many ways, is a byproduct of understanding and accepting oneself—warts and all. Recognizing our strengths just as clearly as our areas for growth makes us more resilient in the face of adversity. Every setback becomes a lesson, every success a validation of our journey, all stemming from a deep root of self-awareness.

Elevated Job Satisfaction

Job satisfaction isn't just about the role we play but also about how that role resonates with our personal values. When the two align, work becomes less of a chore and more of a passion. The days become purpose-driven, challenges turn into opportunities, and the workspace evolves into an arena of growth and fulfillment.

Superior Leadership Skills

Effective leadership is as much about understanding oneself as it is about understanding one's team. A leader who is self-aware can tap into team dynamics in a nuanced way, fostering an environment of trust and mutual respect. It's this blend of personal insight and outward understanding that shapes leaders who are not only respected but also revered.

Self-awareness might seem like a personal endeavor, but its impact is profoundly universal. From shaping our individual journeys to influencing those around us, its reach is both deep and wide. It's not just about knowing oneself but about leveraging that knowledge to craft a life of meaning, purpose, and impact.

Techniques to Enhance Self-Awareness

Developing self-awareness is a lifelong endeavor, but the effort put into understanding oneself can yield powerful insights and growth. By nurturing this skill, we pave the way for more intentional living, improved relationships, and greater clarity in decision-making. Here's a deeper dive into ten techniques that can significantly boost self-awareness:

- **Keep an open mind:** Adopting an open-minded approach allows us to absorb diverse viewpoints and experiences. This acceptance can enrich our perspective and lead to more informed decisions. In a rapidly changing world, an open mind can be our best asset, ensuring adaptability and understanding (Cherry, 2023).
- **Be mindful of your strengths and weaknesses:** A well-rounded self-awareness requires acknowledgment of both strengths and areas of improvement. Celebrating our strengths boosts confidence while understanding our weaknesses provides opportunities for growth. Such balance fosters resilience, adaptability, and a genuine drive for self-improvement (Goleman, 2021).
- **Stay focused:** With so many distractions around, maintaining focus is essential for introspection. By dedicating time to reflect on our goals, values, and actions, we can uncover patterns and behaviors that define us. This dedicated reflection, free from distractions, acts as a mirror, revealing our true selves and guiding our future actions (Wallbridge, 2023).
- **Set boundaries:** Establishing boundaries is vital for mental and emotional well-being. It helps delineate our personal space, ensuring we don't spread ourselves too thin. With clear boundaries, we safeguard our energy,

prioritize our well-being, and gain clarity about our needs and limits (Eurich, 2018).

- **Know your emotional triggers:** Recognizing our emotional triggers is the first step toward proactive emotional management. By identifying these triggers, we can preemptively strategize and avoid reactive behaviors. Understanding these emotional catalysts provides a level of control, enabling more rational responses even in heated situations (Eurich, 2018).

- **Embrace your intuition:** Intuition, often dubbed our "gut feeling," can offer insights that rational thought might miss. Trusting this instinctual knowledge can guide us in situations where data is limited or unclear. Cultivating and heeding our intuition adds another dimension to our decision-making arsenal, often leading to more holistic choices (Eurich, 2018).

- **Practice self-discipline:** Self-discipline shapes our actions and decisions, ensuring they align with our core values. By exercising control over impulses and making deliberate choices, we affirm our commitment to our goals. This commitment, coupled with regular reflection, fosters genuine growth and personal development (Wallbridge, 2023.).

- **Consider how your actions affect others:** Understanding the broader impact of our actions promotes empathy and community-mindedness. It's a reminder that we're part of an interconnected web and that our choices ripple beyond our immediate surroundings. This broader view nurtures compassionate choices and fosters deeper, more understanding relationships (Wallbridge, 2023).

- **Seek feedback:** Gathering feedback offers a window into how others perceive us. While self-reflection is vital, external perspectives can reveal blind spots and areas of growth. Embracing this feedback, especially from trusted sources, can lead to a richer, more well-rounded self-awareness (Eurich, 2018).

- **Engage in continuous learning:** Self-awareness is not a stagnant skill; it evolves with time and experience. Seeking new knowledge, experiences, and perspectives ensures our self-understanding remains current and relevant. As we continue to learn and grow, our self-awareness deepens, making the journey even more rewarding (Betz, 2022).

As we navigate the complexities of life, self-awareness emerges as a guiding light, illuminating our path and choices. By adopting and integrating these techniques, we commit to a life of intentionality, empathy, and genuine growth. It's a commitment that promises not only personal rewards but also a positive impact on the world around us.

IDENTIFYING YOUR EMOTIONAL TRIGGERS

Emotions play a pivotal role in our daily interactions and experiences. While they can elevate our joys and deepen our connections, they can also sometimes take us by surprise, often due to specific triggers. Identifying these triggers is essential in managing our emotional responses and fostering a deeper understanding of ourselves.

What Is an Emotional Trigger?

An emotional trigger, often referred to as a mental trigger, is any topic, event, or situation that consistently evokes a strong emotional response, whether it's sadness, anger, or anxiety. It might not always align with what the majority would perceive as a standard response to the given stimulus. For instance, while one person might find joy in a particular song due to a positive memory associated with it, another person might find it saddening because it reminds them of a challenging time in their life. It's these personalized, often deep-seated connections that bring about intense emotional reactions (Miller, 2020).

Steps to Identifying an Emotional Trigger

- **Stay attuned to your feelings:** The first step is recognizing when you have a stronger emotional reaction than expected. Pay close attention to sudden feelings of discomfort, anger, sadness, or anxiety. These emotions are indicators that you've encountered a trigger.
- **Reflect on the cause:** Once you recognize the emotion, try to understand the root cause. What was happening when you felt that surge of emotion? Was it a comment someone made, a place, or maybe an anniversary of an event? Dig deep and try to connect the dots between the stimulus and your emotional response.

- **Keep a journal:** Documenting instances when you feel triggered can be enlightening. Over time, patterns might emerge, revealing specific triggers. This written record not only helps in identification but also in devising strategies to manage or avoid certain triggers.
- **Seek feedback:** Sometimes, an external perspective can offer invaluable insights. Talk to someone you trust about your reactions. They might have observed patterns or triggers that you haven't noticed.
- **Practice mindfulness:** Engaging in mindfulness exercises can heighten your self-awareness. It allows you to be present, making it easier to spot triggers as they occur. This immediate recognition can often reduce the intensity of the emotional response.

Understanding and identifying our emotional triggers is a significant step toward self-awareness and emotional intelligence. By being proactive in this journey, we equip ourselves with tools to navigate the complexities of our emotional landscape, ensuring our reactions are both understood and manageable.

JOURNALING EXERCISES FOR SELF-REFLECTION

Unearthing the deeper layers of our mind requires introspection, and what better way to dive into this than through journaling? Journaling helps us pause, reflect, and gain insight into our emotions, dreams, and aspirations. Remember, journaling can look different for everyone. To help you embark on this transformative journey, here are a series of exercises:

- **Gratitude list:** Kickstart your mornings by jotting down the everyday joys you encounter. This simple act can help shift your focus toward the positives, grounding you in a mindset of appreciation.
- **Envision the future:** Where do you see yourself a few years from now? Describe that place, those emotions, and the path you'd take to get there. Periodically revisiting this vision can help steer your present actions.
- **Past reflection:** Revisit the turning points in your life. How did those events shape you? Recognizing the lessons from our past can guide our future steps.
- **Current feelings:** Dive into your present emotions. What's bubbling beneath the surface today? By understanding our current state of mind, we can navigate our day more consciously.
- **Self-compassion letter:** We often need reminders of our worth. Write an uplifting letter to yourself, highlighting your strengths and offering gentle encouragement.
- **Life's highs and lows:** Plot out the emotional journey of your past month or year. What events or moments stood out? Reflecting on these can provide a balanced perspective on life's roller coaster.
- **Describe your ideal day:** Paint a picture of a perfect day from dawn to dusk. What would it entail? By dreaming about our ideal scenarios, we get a clearer sense of our desires and values.
- **Conversations with your future self:** Engage in a dialogue with the person you aspire to be. What

wisdom would this future self share? Such an exercise can offer a fresh perspective on present challenges.

- **Personal values:** Pen down the core values that guide your decisions. How did they influence your recent choices? Revisiting these values ensures our actions are consistently aligned with our beliefs.
- **Face your fears:** Confront the shadows lurking in your mind. Describe them, dissect them, and challenge them. Addressing our fears head-on can diminish their hold on us.
- **Personal achievements:** List out your proud moments, however big or small. How did they make you feel? Celebrating our victories instills confidence and motivation.
- **Dream analysis:** Recall a recent dream and dissect its themes and emotions. Dreams can offer unexpected insights into our subconscious, shedding light on suppressed feelings or desires.

Committing to the practice of journaling invites clarity and growth. With each written word, we gain a deeper understanding of our inner world, helping us shape a life that resonates with our true selves.

The Mirror Exercise: Seeing Yourself Through Another's Eyes

One insightful technique for building self-awareness is what I call the "mirror exercise." This involves envisioning yourself from another person's perspective and considering how they might describe you. The goal is to step outside your own biases and see yourself through an objective lens. Here are some steps for this reflective practice:

- **Choose your "mirror."** This could be a close friend, family member, colleague, or even a stranger who has observed you. Select someone who can provide an honest, thoughtful perspective on how you come across.
- **Imagine seeing yourself through their eyes.** Try to set aside your own judgments and self-perceptions. Adopt their vantage point and consider how they might describe your personality, habits, speech patterns, body language, and other tendencies.
- **Note your observations.** Jot down descriptive words and phrases they might use. Don't filter or edit the descriptions—the goal is raw objectivity. Pay attention to both positive and critical observations.
- **Look for alignment and disconnects.** Compare their imagined narrative to your self-perceptions. Are there overlaps or contradictions? What insights emerge from seeing yourself mirrored back in this way?
- **Ask for actual feedback.** To gain an added layer of insight, you could ask your chosen "mirror" for feedback on how they actually perceive you. Compare their real impressions to the ones you imagined.
- **Integrate new perspectives.** Use any eye-opening observations to build greater self-understanding. Look for ways to retain beneficial qualities and evolve areas that need work.

Regularly practicing this exercise with different "mirrors" provides invaluable external perspectives we often overlook. It sheds light on our blind spots and gives a well-rounded view of how the world sees us. Over time, these objective insights help us grow into our best and most self-aware selves.

Exploring Your Core Values Through Reflection

Our values serve as an inner compass, guiding our choices and behaviors. But in the rush of daily life, they often fade into the background. Intentionally identifying and reflecting on your core values provides clarity and focus. Here are some useful exercises:

- Review your recent decisions—what values influenced them? Look for recurring themes to reveal your priorities.
- Imagine your 80th birthday party—what would you want people to describe as your values?
- Write your ideal obituary and consider what values you'd want highlighted.
- Make two lists—moments when you felt happiest and most distressed. What values were present or missing?
- If you could instill one value in your children, what would it be? Why?
- What qualities do you admire most in your role models or heroes? Do you embody those values?
- When have you compromised your values? How did it impact you? What values were neglected?

- Which daily activities align with your values? Which feel disconnected?
- If you could have a billboard anywhere, what value would you promote on it?
- What principles guide your friendships and relationships?

Regular value reflection provides a compass when you feel adrift and clarity when faced with difficult choices. It's an empowering practice for gaining self-awareness.

Cultivating Self-Compassion

In our quest for self-awareness, we must not only understand our strengths and weaknesses—but embrace them with compassion. Self-compassion entails treating ourselves with care, concern, and understanding—especially during difficult times. When integrated as part of self-awareness, it provides:

- A buffer against self-criticism and negative self-talk. With self-compassion, we counterbalance constructive self-reflection with kindness.
- Greater emotional resilience. Self-compassion helps us cope with challenging emotions, failures, and setbacks with wisdom and grace.
- Deeper self-motivation. We avoid destructive perfectionism and speak to ourselves as we would a close friend—with encouragement.
- Healthier boundaries. Self-compassion teaches us to say no when needed and prioritize our well-being.

- Enhanced self-care. We make self-compassion actionable through soothing activities like meditation, yoga, and journaling.
- More courage to be vulnerable. By embracing our imperfections, we open ourselves to authentic human connection.
- Increased empathy. Accepting our own flaws allows for a deeper understanding of others.

Practical Tips for Self-Compassion:

- Notice self-judgmental thoughts and consciously reframe them with gentleness.
- Treat yourself with the caring actions and words you would show a friend in need.
- Recall a time you felt comforted and channel that feeling toward yourself.
- Write a heartfelt letter to yourself expressing understanding for your flaws.
- Imagine yourself as a child and provide the care your inner child needs.
- Ask: Would I say this to someone I love? If not, don't say it to yourself.
- See failures as opportunities for growth, not condemnation.
- Surround yourself with those who reinforce your intrinsic self-worth.

With its ethos of wisdom and care for oneself, self-compassion provides the nourishing soil for self-awareness to take root and blossom into its fullest, most beautiful expression.

The Art of Receiving Feedback

Our blind spots obscure what is clear to others. Feedback offers an invaluable external mirror into our impact and behaviors. But beyond simply receiving feedback, we must learn to accept it gracefully and integrate it constructively. Here are some best practices:

- **Listen openly:** Avoid knee-jerk defensiveness. Create a safe space for the feedback giver to speak honestly and be fully heard. Offer your complete presence.
- **Ask reflective questions:** Seek to understand their perspective fully. Ask for specific examples or clarification. Inquire about the feelings evoked or needs being unmet.
- **Express appreciation:** Thank them for caring enough and risking discomfort to share this gift of insight with you. Appreciate their courage.
- **Consider carefully:** Reflect deeply on the feedback over time. What core truth rings clear? How can this elevate your self-awareness?
- **Integrate selectively:** Not all feedback warrants change. Consider the source and their motive. Determine what rings true. Let the rest go.

- **Enact mindfully:** If the feedback reveals a blind spot needing attention, brainstorm small mindful steps. Don't try changing everything overnight.
- **Circle back:** Once you've had time to integrate, follow up with the giver. Share your appreciation again, along with your game plan for growth.

This form of receptive, discerning openness to feedback cultivates self-awareness. Our critics can become our teachers when we develop the courage to listen, reflect, and grow.

WRAPPING UP

Looking back to the insight from Marshall B. Rosenberg about the responsibility tied to our actions and feelings, it's evident just how pivotal self-awareness is in our lives. This expanded chapter has provided additional tools and understanding to navigate your emotional terrain with greater confidence.

We've now covered the following:

- a deep dive into what self-awareness truly means and why it's crucial
- the wide-ranging benefits that come from being in tune with oneself
- practical steps and reflective exercises to enrich your self-awareness
- ways to receive feedback and cultivate self-compassion on the journey

With this strengthened foundation of self-understanding, we can craft lives of deeper purpose, wisdom, and compassion. As we turn the page, we'll carry these lessons forward, exploring the intricacies of resilience and how self-awareness equips us to thrive.

CASE STUDY: JACK

Meet Jack. He was a middle school teacher in a small suburban community. His work was demanding, both emotionally and intellectually. He was the kind of teacher who wouldn't just teach algebra but would also delve into the emotional lives of his students. Yet, despite his best intentions, his classroom dynamics were shaky. Why? Jack himself couldn't put a finger on it. Until he decided that the place to start wasn't with his students; it was with himself. The realm of self-awareness.

With courage as his compass, Jack started exploring what self-awareness actually meant. It wasn't a self-indulgent navel-gazing exercise but a multidimensional lens through which he learned to see his thoughts, emotions, and actions. He started with introspection but extended it to be receptive to feedback, even when it was tough to hear. The multiple facets of his character started revealing themselves, and he realized that self-awareness was not just knowing himself but also understanding how he was perceived by others. It was like a song; it wasn't enough to just know the lyrics; you needed to hear how it sounded to others.

Jack became aware of his emotional patterns, the triggers that took him off course. He started recognizing that his irritability wasn't because his students were challenging but because he was stressed about aging parents, a mortgage, and life's other curveballs. With this newfound awareness, he found he was better able to manage his reactions, his communication sharpened, and his relationships deepened. His students began to trust him more, and even his personal relationships bloomed. Self-awareness had made him a happier person, a more fulfilled teacher, and a more supportive friend and family member.

Committed to staying on this transformative path, Jack deployed a range of techniques to hone his self-awareness. He started journaling, capturing his thoughts, feelings, and a-ha moments. He practiced mindfulness, observing his thoughts without judgment. He even learned to set boundaries, recognizing that self-care wasn't selfish but essential for balanced living. One of his most transformative practices was identifying his emotional triggers. For Jack, it was the sense of not being heard, stemming from his childhood. Recognizing this allowed him to navigate emotional landscapes—both his and others— with far greater ease.

Journaling became Jack's go-to tool for reflection. He scribbled down his worries, his aspirations, and even his daily mundane interactions. And every time he did, he found a piece of himself in those ink marks. It was like each entry brought clarity, like wiping a foggy windowpane until he could see clearly. As he journaled, he understood himself better and, in doing so, understood his students, friends, and loved ones more deeply. too.

So, circling back to where we began, the lack of self-awareness wasn't just a personal deficit; it was a relational one. The responsibility for how we behaved, thought, and felt didn't just impact us; it rippled into every life we touched. And just like Jack, it was this awakening that not only helped us live authentically but elevated our very humanness. You weren't just gaining insight into how you ticked, but you were also acquiring the ability to engage with the world in a way that was transformative.

CASE STUDY: SAM

You know, it's funny how life has a way of pushing us to make changes, right? Take Sam, for example, a 35-year-old guy who'd been feeling like something was missing for years. He wasn't unhappy, per se, but he often felt disconnected—from his job, from his friends, and even from Tracy, his long-time partner.

One evening, he and Tracy had one of those arguments— you know, the kind that makes you stop and question things. The kind that makes you think, *How did we get here?* It was in that moment of reflection that he stumbled upon a book about emotional intelligence and got curious about this thing called self-awareness. Like, what does that even mean?

So, Sam figured he'd give it a go. He bought a journal—nothing fancy, just a notebook—and started jotting down what he felt each day, what ticked him off, what made him happy, all that good stuff. It didn't take long before he noticed a pattern. Work stress was his kryptonite. If he had a bad day at the office, you bet it would spill into his home life.

Realizing that was a game-changer, he thought, *I've got to handle this stress thing better.* That's when he took up mindfulness. Now, this isn't some mystical thing; he simply started taking short breaks to breathe, clear his head, that sort of thing. He even signed up for a meditation class.

And you won't believe the ripple effect this had. At work, Sam found he was making better choices. He was like a stress detective, catching himself before stress could muddle his thinking. He even noticed he was getting along better with his colleagues. Who would've thought?

But here's the real kicker: his relationship with Tracy? Night and day difference. They still had their disagreements—hey, who doesn't?—but now, Sam was a lot better at saying what was actually bothering him. No more shouting matches: they'd sit, talk, and most of the time, figure things out.

He started feeling better about pretty much everything. His days felt purposeful, and he was genuinely happier. It's as if the fog lifted and he could see the world more clearly. The best part? He knew exactly what was important to him, and that made it easier to invest time in the things—and people—that really mattered.

A year into this whole self-discovery adventure, Sam couldn't believe the change. It wasn't just about understanding himself better; it was like he had this toolset for dealing with life's ups and downs. So, yeah, Sam's story is one of those real-life testimonies to how making a commitment to understanding yourself can seriously upgrade your life—be it your job, your relationships, or just your own peace of mind.

3

STEP #3—BUILDING EMOTIONAL RESILIENCE

> *We cannot tell what may happen to us in the strange medley of life. But we can decide what happens in us — how we can take it, what we do with it — and that is what really counts in the end.*
>
> — JOSEPH FORT NEWTON

This insightful quote perfectly captures the spirit of what this chapter is all about. Life's curveballs are inevitable, but our reactions to them are entirely up to us. So, how do we ensure that our internal responses are as constructive as possible? That's where emotional resilience comes into play. With this skill in your toolbox, you're not just weathering life's storms; you're learning how to dance in the rain.

Welcome to Chapter 3, where we're tackling the robust subject of emotional resilience head-on. Think of this skill as your personal shield against life's trials and tribulations. The core idea here is not just about "making it through" but truly flourishing no matter what comes your way. The aim? To unlock your ability to bounce back from adversity effortlessly and with newfound wisdom.

The focus of this chapter goes beyond mere survival. It's about prospering. Whether you're navigating office politics, juggling personal responsibilities, or dealing with downright tough times, resilience equips you to face these challenges, grow from them, and come out the other side stronger than ever.

UNDERSTANDING EMOTIONAL RESILIENCE

You might hear this term and think it's some sort of emotional superhero cape we can throw on to dodge life's bullets. But it's not about that, not at all. Emotional resilience is less about dodging and more about showing up in your life, challenges and all.

Consider the experience of losing a client at work. It's easy to plunge into a whirlpool of self-doubt and negativity. But if you're practicing emotional resilience, you acknowledge the pain without getting consumed by it. You say to yourself, "This hurts, but what can I learn from it? How can I evolve?" You're not shoving emotions aside; you're looking them in the eye and asking them what they have to teach you.

Or imagine you've just gone through a gut-wrenching breakup. Emotional resilience doesn't mean plastering a fake smile on your face and declaring you're fine. No. It means allowing yourself to feel the ache in your heart while also knowing this is a chapter, not your entire book. It means asking yourself, "How can I heal in a way that respects my feelings but also leads me to growth?" You lean into the discomfort just enough to come out stronger on the other end.

And let's be clear: This isn't just motivational fluff. Emotional resilience is grounded in a rich bedrock of research (Fritz et al., 2018) that touches on emotional well-being, mental health, and general life satisfaction. It's the real deal.

So, here's the bottom line: Emotional resilience is not about skating over life's challenges or denying your emotions. It's about fully engaging with your life—messy parts and all—and making conscious choices about how you respond to adversity. It's not about becoming emotion-proof; it's about becoming emotion-wise.

Benefits of Emotional Resilience

What do you get out of emotional resilience? Because, let's face it, if you're going to invest your heart and soul into developing this skill, you want to know it's worth it. And let me tell you, the benefits are manifold and they hit you right where you live: in your relationships, your workplace, and deep inside that beautiful mess we call the human psyche.

First up, emotional resilience is your golden ticket to better mental health. We're talking less anxiety, less depression, and a real boost to your general mood. When life tries to knock you down, emotional resilience helps you get back up with your dignity intact. And the cool part? The stronger your emotional resilience, the less likely you are to get knocked down in the first place.

Now, let's talk about relationships—arguably the meat and potatoes of life. Emotional resilience helps you cultivate deeper, more authentic connections. It's like you have this emotional toolkit, and when misunderstandings or conflicts arise, instead of throwing your hands up, you're like, "I got this." You dig into that toolkit and pull out empathy, active listening, and constructive communication. So, instead of driving people away, you're drawing them closer.

And what about your professional life? Imagine walking into a high-stakes meeting or negotiation. With emotional resilience, you're not a ball of stress; you're centered. Even if the conversation goes south, you maintain your poise and navigate through the storm without losing sight of your goals. You're not just surviving your workday; you're owning it.

Here's another nugget of truth: Emotional resilience even plays into your physical well-being. Yes, you heard me right. Stress takes a toll on the body, but resilience acts like a shield. It's associated with lower rates of illness and quicker recovery times. Your body and mind are intrinsically linked, and emotional resilience nurtures that connection.

And you don't have to take my word for it. A wealth of research supports these benefits, from improved mental well-being to enhanced relationship quality and even better physical health. Science backs this up as solidly as a sturdy oak tree.

Emotional resilience is not some abstract, nice-to-have quality. It's a game-changer. It's what equips you to live your life fully, with a heart wide open to both joys and challenges. And let me tell you, living life in full color like that is something you don't want to miss.

STRATEGIES FOR COPING WITH STRESS AND ADVERSITY

The reality of life is that we all encounter hardships, obstacles, and stressors. This is where good coping skills become invaluable. They serve as a protective shield, enabling us to manage life's challenges with resilience and composure. These coping abilities don't just save us from emotional turbulence; they also have profound implications for our physical well-being, guarding against stress-induced health problems. With coping skills at your disposal, you gain the mental clarity and focus required to function optimally in your personal and professional life.

How to Cope With Stress and Adversity

To understand the true essence of coping, it's important to start with self-awareness. Recognizing when you're stressed isn't as simple as it sounds. Whether it manifests as physical sensations like a racing heart or emotional states like feeling overwhelmed, the key is to identify these stress signals early on. Once you do, techniques like deep breathing or even taking a brief walk can alter your emotional landscape.

Another cornerstone of effective coping involves shifting your perspective. During a crisis, it's easy to blow things out of proportion. A moment of pause to ask yourself, "Will this matter in a year? Or in five years?" can drastically alter your emotional response and help you keep the larger picture in view.

Don't underestimate the role of social support, either. A meaningful conversation with a trusted friend or family member can provide not just emotional relief, but often insights and solutions as well. Sometimes, sharing your burden can make it feel lighter.

But what about those times when facing the issue head-on feels too intense? It's completely all right to distract yourself briefly. Healthy distractions like reading, a warm bath, or watching a favorite TV show can be like emotional pit stops, giving you the energy to face your challenges afresh.

Then, there's the empowering act of problem-solving. Instead of dwelling on the problem, direct your mental energy toward devising practical solutions. You can start by breaking down the problem into smaller tasks and addressing them individually. This proactive approach can give you a sense of control, even when circumstances seem uncontrollable.

It's also crucial to challenge and reassess your thoughts. Cognitive reappraisal, where you consciously alter your interpretation of stressful situations, can be remarkably effective. You can train yourself to reframe your thoughts in a way that reduces emotional distress.

Finally, there's no shame in seeking professional help. Sometimes, our own coping strategies fall short, and that's when the guidance of a qualified expert can make a world of difference.

So, in essence, learning to cope is a continuous process. As you improve your coping skills, you'll find you're not just surviving, but thriving—living a life that is as fulfilling as it is resilient.

UNDERSTANDING THE CONNECTION BETWEEN EMOTIONAL INTELLIGENCE AND GROWTH MINDSET

If we look at emotional intelligence and growth mindset as two friends sitting in a coffee shop, deep in meaningful conversation, we'll see how intertwined they really are. Emotional intelligence is that friend who truly listens, not just to us but to everyone around them. It's the friend who helps us recognize and name our feelings. With emotional intelligence, we're not just responding to life; we're really living it, feeling our way through it. This sets the stage for its coffee shop companion—a growth mindset. A growth mindset is our friend who nudges us to see every stumble as a setup for a leap. Together, they're a pair that inspires us to see challenges as chances, not just trials to endure but opportunities to soar.

Growth Mindset vs. Fixed Mindset

When we think of mindsets, we often place them into two boxes: fixed and growth. A fixed mindset whispers that our talents and capabilities are pre-determined. It's like saying, "This is the hand you're dealt. Deal with it." It's a storyline that many of us know too well. But there's another narrative, one of expansion and possibilities—that's a growth mindset. This mindset isn't just about proving how smart or talented we are; it's about stretching, evolving, and discovering what we're capable of. You know, the delicious realization that we're more elastic than static.

Benefits of a Growth Mindset

Ever think about what's in it for you when you start looking at life through the lens of a growth mindset? Besides the obvious benefits like becoming a more adaptable and engaging human being? A growth mindset doesn't just make you resilient; it makes you alive to change, less defensive, and more open. It's like having a sturdy yet supple backbone that supports you as you take risks and explore the unknown. You become not just the student but also the teacher, and your world grows larger. The ripple effect touches your relationships and your work, enriching them in ways that you might not have expected but will definitely appreciate.

Strategies for Developing a Growth Mindset

So, how do you foster this mindset that champions growth? It starts by understanding that challenges are less about confronting roadblocks and more about welcoming signposts. These signposts guide you toward personal development, not divert you from it. Embracing a sense of persistence is key here, but don't mistake this for stubbornness. It's about resiliently holding onto your goals while being flexible about how to reach them. A huge part of the journey is self-reflection, that quiet space where you digest the good, the bad, and the insightful. It's the introspective moment where you recognize what's within your control and accept what's not, only to find a new way forward. Feeling a bit uncomfortable is just a signal that you're stepping into your growth zone, and trust me, that's exactly where you want to be.

EXERCISES FOR BUILDING EMOTIONAL STRENGTH

Navigating life's ups and downs requires more than just mental acuity; it calls for emotional strength, a kind of resilience that allows us to cope, adapt, and thrive in the face of challenges. You can't always control what happens to you, but you certainly can control how you react. Emotional resilience isn't an inherent trait; it's a skill, and like any skill, it can be developed and refined. In this section, we're going to explore practical, everyday exercises to build your emotional strength. These are your tools; consider them your emotional first-aid kit. They're designed to not only equip you with immediate coping mechanisms but also to instill a lasting mental fortitude. Each exercise is a stepping stone on the path to a more resilient you. Let's get started.

Mindful Observation

Instructions:

- Find a quiet, comfortable space to sit or stand.
- Choose an object within your line of sight.
- Take a deep breath and focus solely on this object for 2–5 minutes.

Mindful observation is a form of meditation that sharpens your ability to concentrate and builds emotional steadiness. By directing your focus toward one object, you train your brain to screen out distractions, making you less susceptible to emotional spirals triggered by outside stressors. It also teaches you to find solace in simplicity, a valuable skill when the world around you seems chaotic. Not to mention, it's a form of grounding that can be used anytime, anywhere. You can even use this technique during stressful work situations by simply focusing on an object on your desk or a feature in the room.

The "AND" Technique

Instructions:

- Identify a strong emotion you're currently feeling.
- Say to yourself, "I'm feeling [emotion] AND..."
- Complete the sentence with another emotion or thought you are also experiencing.

The "AND" Technique is based on the idea that we are capable of feeling more than one emotion simultaneously. It discourages black-and-white thinking, a cognitive distortion that often fuels anxiety and depression. This method encourages you to accept that you can feel anxious AND optimistic or happy AND uncertain. Embracing this emotional duality creates space for nuanced self-reflection, equipping you with a balanced emotional outlook. This practice can be particularly useful in high-stakes situations like job interviews or challenging conversations where emotional clarity can make a significant difference.

Three Good Things

Instructions:

- At the end of each day, take out a notebook or open a digital document.
- Write down three positive things that happened during the day.
- Reflect on each one, even elaborating on why it was important to you.

The power of gratitude can't be overstated. By focusing on what went well, you foster a positive mind frame, which can be a buffer against stress and negativity. Not only does this make you more resilient in the face of adversity, but it also makes your joys more sustainable. Over time, this habit can change your brain's default setting from one of apprehension to one of appreciation, which has long-term benefits for your mental health. Moreover, this practice has the potential to positively influence your relationships, as you'll find yourself acknowledging and appreciating the good in others as well.

The Self-Compassion Letter

Instructions:

- Sit in a quiet space with a pen and paper or a digital writing tool.
- Write a letter to yourself addressing a current challenge or difficulty you're facing.
- Write as if you were talking to a dear friend who is going through the same issue.

It's easy to be hard on ourselves, particularly when facing challenges. Self-compassion is the often-overlooked counterpart to self-esteem. While self-esteem asks, "How can I be better?" self-compassion asks, "How can I be kinder to myself in this moment?" Writing a self-compassion letter allows you to step out of your situation and view it from an external perspective, offering you insights you might have overlooked. This exercise can be an emotional lifeline, giving you the support and courage to take constructive action.

Creative Expression

Instructions:

- Choose a medium you enjoy—drawing, writing, cooking, playing music, and so on.
- Dedicate some uninterrupted time to engage in this creative activity.
- Allow your emotions to flow into what you're creating.

Sometimes, words alone can't capture the full spectrum of our emotions. Engaging in a creative endeavor can act as a cathartic release for emotions that are too complex to articulate. It's a form of self-therapy, allowing you to interpret your feelings without judgment or the need to make sense of them immediately. Over time, you'll find that this exercise not only releases pent-up emotions but also brings you a sense of peace and achievement.

These exercises serve as your emotional gym, and like any form of exercise, the benefits compound over time. What starts as a daily effort will eventually become second nature, transforming not just how you handle adversity, but also how you live your everyday life. It's all about daily commitment, a willingness to confront your emotional blind spots, and the courage to improve and grow stronger.

WRAPPING UP

We began this journey with a poignant reminder from Joseph Fort Newton (n.d.): "We cannot tell what may happen to us in the strange medley of life. But we can decide what happens in us—how we can take it, what we do with it—and that is what really counts in the end." You've taken substantial steps toward making what counts, well, truly count.

In this chapter, you've learned

- what emotional resilience is and why it's essential.
- strategies for coping with stress and adversity.
- the importance of a growth mindset in fostering emotional resilience.
- tangible exercises to build emotional strength.

Each of these aspects works in concert to form a well-rounded, emotionally resilient individual. You're learning to be the master of your emotional domain, someone who can not only withstand life's challenges but flourish in spite of them.

But mastering emotional resilience is just one piece of a larger puzzle. It sets the stage for deeper emotional intelligence, a skill set that's essential for living a fulfilling life. Intrigued? Good, because our next chapter dives into Step #4: Cultivating Emotional Intelligence. It's one you won't want to miss as we continue to build upon the sturdy foundation you've already laid.

CASE STUDY: EMMA

Emma, a single mother of two, found her world turned upside down with a turbulent divorce and job loss in the wake of an economic downturn. Feeling the weight of these challenges, she found solace in the words of Joseph Fort Newton: "We cannot tell what may happen to us in the strange medley of life. But we can decide what happens in us—how we can take it, what we do with it—and that is what really counts in the end." These words became her guide as she made the conscious decision not just to weather her storms, but to emerge stronger.

In the darkest moments, Emma discovered that emotional resilience was not merely a trait but a dynamic process. She realized it was her ability to adapt and bounce back that empowered her to face life's adversities. She saw herself as a willow tree, bending under strong winds but not breaking. This understanding of emotional resilience came to light not through avoidance but by confronting life's challenges head-on. She leveraged this understanding to cultivate improved coping mechanisms, fortify her relationships, and build a deeper trust in her ability to navigate future life challenges.

Emma realized that emotional strength was not just about enduring hardship but about intelligently navigating through it. She began to see coping skills as her emotional GPS, directing her through the complex terrain of stress and challenges. By identifying her stress triggers and adopting mindfulness practices, she gained control over her emotional responses. She also realized the importance of physical well-being to emotional health and engaged in regular exercise, complemented by professional guidance to manage her emotional landscape more effectively.

As Emma honed her emotional intelligence, she observed a shift in her mindset. She found a strong connection between emotional intelligence and a growth mindset. No longer did she view her setbacks as limitations; they became learning opportunities. The intersection of emotional intelligence and a growth mindset led Emma to a more adaptable and eager approach to life's challenges. She found that her resilience expanded, allowing her to bounce back from setbacks more easily. Through constant reflection, she gradually changed her outlook, embracing life's challenges as opportunities for growth.

To further enhance her emotional resilience, Emma embraced daily practices that seemed simple but were profoundly impactful. For instance, she would engage in a "Why Ladder," a form of self-dialogue where she would repeatedly ask herself 'why' to reach the root cause of her emotional state. She also practiced emotional role-playing, a method where she would mentally rehearse how to respond to different emotional triggers. Another significant practice was maintaining a gratitude journal, which dramatically improved her perspective by focusing on positive aspects of her life.

CASE STUDY: ERICKA

Ericka was a powerhouse in the realm of corporate finance, her reputation preceding her in boardrooms across the city. However, when a difficult breakup coincided with unprecedented challenges at work, the walls she had so skillfully built started to crack. Ericka felt lost, with a constant feeling of overwhelm gnawing at her. During a layover at an airport, she picked up a book similar to this one on emotional resilience, almost as if guided by intuition.

As she turned the pages, Ericka felt an immediate connection to the concept. Emotional resilience wasn't about suppressing emotions or slapping on a smile to face the world. It was about the capacity to rebound from setbacks and to adapt in the face of adversity. What struck Ericka was the realization that resilience was the secret sauce to maintaining not only her professional acumen but also her emotional well-being in personal relationships.

Keen to explore this further, she dove into research on effective coping strategies. Gone were the days of drowning her sorrows in wine or losing herself in back-to-back episodes of TV series. Ericka took up mindfulness and meditation. The simple act of focusing on her breath and centering her thoughts allowed her a newfound clarity. She learned to confront, rather than avoid, her stressors, taking them apart piece by piece to better understand and manage them. It wasn't a quick fix, but rather a journey to building an inner arsenal to weather life's ups and downs.

While on this voyage of self-discovery, Ericka also stumbled upon the concept of a growth mindset. It was as if someone had finally put into words what she had long felt but couldn't articulate. The idea of viewing challenges as stepping stones rather than stumbling blocks was transformative. Instead of being shackled by the fear of failure, she embraced it as a learning opportunity, finding value even in the setbacks. Ericka saw how this shift was essential not only for her professional life but for personal growth and emotional well-being, too.

As months turned into a year, the results were nothing short of remarkable. The same job that had once been a constant source of stress became a playground for her newfound resilience and growth mindset. She tackled projects with a nuanced perspective, allowing her to navigate complex negotiations with ease. On the personal front, the emotional void left by her breakup began filling with self-love and a greater appreciation for solitude. Ericka even took to journaling as a form of self-expression and reflection, further solidifying her emotionally resilient foundation.

The most impressive part of her transformation, though, was the undeniable domino effect it had on all aspects of her life. Relationships were healthier; her professional life flourished even more, and above all, Ericka found a deep-rooted sense of contentment and joy. The constant anxiety that used to cloud her thoughts like a lingering fog had lifted, replaced by the sunny skies of emotional freedom.

Ericka's journey wasn't just a series of fortunate events or a lucky break; it was a calculated, conscious effort to develop a skill set that ultimately reshaped her world. So, if you're standing at the edge, wondering how to traverse the choppy waters of life, channel Ericka and live your best life.

4

STEP #4—ENHANCING YOUR SOCIAL SKILLS

> *We plant seeds that will flower as results in our lives, so best to remove the weeds of anger, avarice, envy, and doubt...*

— DOROTHY DAY

The wisdom of Dorothy Day serves as a gentle reminder that our actions and interactions carry long-lasting repercussions, shaping the quality of our lives and those around us. Just as a gardener carefully tends to each bud, leaf, and stem, we, too, must cultivate our social skills to yield a harvest rich in meaningful connections, self-understanding, and collective well-being.

Welcome to Step #4: Enhancing Your Social Skills. Here, we'll confront some of the most common obstacles you may face in interpersonal situations and provide practical tips for turning awkward moments into opportunities for genuine connection. Our goal? To equip you with the skills necessary for optimized levels of emotional intelligence. By nurturing these skills, you not only improve your life but also sow seeds of kindness, empathy, and understanding in the world around you.

So, if you've ever found yourself tongue-tied at parties, misunderstood in meetings, or simply longing for deeper, more enriching relationships, this chapter is for you. Let's start sowing those seeds and watch how they transform your emotional landscape.

THE RELATIONSHIP BETWEEN SOCIAL SKILLS AND EMOTIONAL INTELLIGENCE

The relationship between social skills and emotional intelligence is deeply intertwined, much like the roots and branches of a sturdy tree. If emotional intelligence is the root system—giving us stability, nourishment, and a strong foundation—then social skills are the branches that reach out into the world, allowing us to connect, communicate, and collaborate effectively with others.

In Daniel Goleman's framework of emotional intelligence, social skills are considered one of the five critical components (Goleman, 2021). They are the outward manifestation of our internal emotional competencies. While other elements like self-awareness, self-regulation, and empathy help us understand and manage our own emotions, social skills translate that internal understanding into external action. They enable us to navigate complex social situations and foster positive relationships, both of which are critical in reaching our personal and professional goals.

Social skills aren't just about making small talk or mastering the art of conversation. They encompass a wide array of competencies like active listening, conflict resolution, and even leadership abilities. These skills, when honed, contribute to higher emotional intelligence as they require a deep understanding of both self and others. In other words, effective social skills require you to tap into your emotional intelligence to perceive, evaluate, and respond to social cues in a way that is both genuine and constructive.

Emotional intelligence and social skills are two sides of the same coin. One is inward-facing, helping us to understand ourselves, while the other is outward-facing, enabling us to engage with the world around us. Together, they create a harmonious cycle where improved emotional intelligence leads to better social skills, and better social skills, in turn, enhance our emotional intelligence. So, as we work on developing one, we invariably enrich the other, creating a life that's both emotionally rewarding and socially fulfilling.

THE IMPORTANCE OF EFFECTIVE COMMUNICATION

Communication is not just a skill; it's an art form. It's not merely a transaction where one person talks and the other listens. It's an interaction, a dialogue where both parties are fully present. So, let's talk about what we mean by effective communication. It's not about using ten-dollar words or mastering the art of persuasion. It's about connecting authentically and being yourself while allowing others the same privilege.

True communication has depth; it's about leaning into the discomfort to say what you mean, but also pausing to really hear what someone else is trying to say. We've all experienced those precious moments when we feel genuinely seen and heard—those are the exchanges that stay with us, the ones that forge bonds and deepen our understanding of not only others but ourselves.

Let's shift the way we think about this. It's not just about "telling and receiving," but rather, it's about "sharing and co-creating." Don't just share your point of view; share yourself. And don't just take in information; become a part of the narrative, share your story, and connect. This doesn't happen overnight; it takes practice and a willingness to mess up and try again. But when we invest in truly understanding this art form, we enrich our own lives and the lives of those around us.

Benefits of Effective Communication

The quality of our relationships, whether at work or home, is often mirrored by the quality of our communication. When you can talk openly, when you can show up authentically and let others do the same, you lay down the bricks for a bridge that's both strong and flexible. This isn't just about knowing when to speak; it's also about knowing when to listen, when to ask questions, and when to simply be there, offering your presence as the most profound form of support. This mutual exchange, this give-and-take, is like a duet that nurtures not just a relationship but individual growth.

Helps Handle Conflicts Better

Conflict. The word alone might make your heart rate jump a little. But what if we saw conflict not as a crisis but as an opportunity? An opportunity to deepen our understanding, to fine-tune our empathy, to refine the edges of our own self-awareness? Effective communication lets us do that. It's the framework that allows us to navigate disagreements with integrity and to hash things out without tearing each other down. It's about leaning into the discomfort, not with armor, but with openness. And when we approach conflict this way, we come out the other side stronger and wiser.

Builds Empathy

If there's one thing we're starved for in this world, it's empathy. We don't just need to recognize it; we need to cultivate it like our lives depend on it—because they do. Empathy is the emotional currency that enriches our inner lives and sweetens our social interactions. Effective communication lets us do more than put ourselves in someone else's shoes—it lets us walk in them. When you truly listen to understand, not just to respond, you're not just hearing words; you're touching a soul. This kind of soul-to-soul connection creates a shared space for true compassion to bloom.

Increases Self-Awareness

The journey toward effective communication is not just outward; it's also inward. As we get better at engaging with others, we simultaneously unveil layers of our own inner world. Self-awareness isn't merely a byproduct of good communication; it's a cornerstone. How can you share yourself authentically if you haven't first confronted your own complexities? The more we know ourselves, the better we communicate, and vice versa.

Builds Trust

Trust is more than just a five-letter word; it's the invisible glue that holds our social fabric together. Trust isn't a commodity you can buy or a favor you can trade. It's earned, and the currency we use is genuine, transparent communication. When you can speak your truth and allow others to speak theirs, when you can disagree without being disagreeable, when you can be vulnerable without feeling weak—that's when trust blossoms. It becomes the solid foundation on which all other virtues can stand.

So, there it is—effective communication is not just a skill to be acquired. It's a path to a richer, more resonant life.

ACTIVE LISTENING TECHNIQUES

Listening isn't just about hearing words. We're all pretty good at nodding while mentally composing our grocery list. But here's the deal—active listening is about creating a spacious room in your mind and inviting someone else's words to come and dance. It's a whole different league from what we call "passive listening," which is that nod-and-smile routine we're all too familiar with.

In passive listening, your ears might catch the sound, but your heart misses the emotion, and your brain misses the nuance. Active listening is an intentional act. You make a deliberate choice to give your undivided attention, to dive into the conversation not as a spectator, but as an engaged participant. It's about making eye contact, providing feedback, and asking probing questions that dig deeper into the discussion. You're not just on the receiving end of communication; you're an active collaborator in the process.

So, why does this matter? Well, active listening isn't just a technique; it's a way of being in the world. It's how you invite more depth into your interactions and how you cultivate that elusive treasure we call "understanding." Whether you're negotiating a contract, deepening a friendship, or trying to see eye-to-eye with a family member, active listening is your best friend. It equips you with the tools to dig for the treasures often buried in the hills of our daily dialogues. So yes, let's aim to do more than just hear. Let's listen—actively.

How to Listen Actively

When you listen actively, you're not just lending an ear; you're lending your whole self. Your mind isn't elsewhere; it's right there, in the conversation. Think about the people who have really listened to you in your life. How did they make you feel? Heard, valued, respected—right? That's the gift you can offer to someone when you truly engage in active listening.

Face the Speaker and Have Eye Contact

The art of active listening starts with positioning yourself to fully engage with the speaker. When you face the speaker and maintain eye contact, you're not just observing; you're participating in the conversation. This simple but intentional action can powerfully communicate that you're present and interested. In turn, it encourages the speaker to be more open, fostering a dialogue that is more genuine and productive. In essence, your body language sets the stage for meaningful communication.

"Listen" to Non-Verbal Cues Too

While spoken words carry the crux of the message, there's a parallel conversation happening through non-verbal cues. Gestures, facial expressions, and even pauses contribute significantly to the message. Being attentive to these subtleties offers you a more nuanced understanding of the discussion. It's like reading between the lines; you get the full story, not just the summary. Your awareness of these cues also shows the speaker that you genuinely care about what they're saying beyond just the words they use.

Don't Interrupt

Resisting the temptation to interrupt is a cornerstone of active listening. Interruptions can disrupt the flow of the conversation and may prevent the speaker from getting to the core of their message. By keeping silent at the right times, you're handing the speaker a figurative microphone, saying, "This is your stage, your moment. I'm here to listen." It's a simple yet profound way to show respect and open-mindedness.

Listen Without Judging or Jumping to Conclusions

When you listen without preconceived judgments or the impulse to draw early conclusions, you create a space where open and honest communication can take place. Imagine your mind as a blank slate, open to various colors and forms. By keeping your internal commentary at bay, you allow the speaker to freely express their thoughts and feelings. You're essentially saying, "I'm here to understand you, not to judge or solve you."

Don't Start Planning What to Say Next

As tempting as it is to plan your next sentence or rebuttal, doing so takes you out of the moment. The magic of active listening lies in genuine presence. By focusing entirely on what's being said, you increase your understanding of the speaker's point of view. You'll also find that when you listen closely, your appropriate response often naturally emerges from the conversation itself without pre-planning.

Don't Impose Your Opinions or Solutions

Even if you think you've got the perfect advice or solution, hold off on sharing it unless you're asked. Offering unsolicited advice can inadvertently send the message that you're not really listening, but rather waiting for your turn to speak. When you listen without imposing your own opinions, you're showing the speaker that their thoughts and feelings are valid, fostering a more supportive environment.

Stay Focused

A wandering mind is a common obstacle to active listening. If you find your attention drifting, gently bring it back to the conversation at hand. Mindfulness techniques, such as focusing on your breath, can be helpful in keeping you anchored. Your focus is a gift to the speaker and yourself; it enriches the conversation and your relationships.

Ask Questions

Inquiring for clarification or elaboration not only shows your interest but can also uncover deeper layers of the topic at hand. It tells the speaker, "I care enough to understand this fully." It's an extension of active listening and adds another dimension to the conversation. Asking questions helps you both dig deeper, turning a superficial chat into a meaningful dialogue.

Practicing these techniques can transform your conversations from mundane exchanges to enriching experiences, bringing benefits that ripple out into all areas of your life.

TYPES OF NON-VERBAL COMMUNICATION

Let's take a moment to appreciate the unspoken dimensions of our conversations—the way our bodies "speak" even when we're silent. Non-verbal communication is the wordless exchange that happens alongside or instead of verbal dialogue. It's a symphony of facial expressions, gestures, eye contact, posture, and even the distance we keep from each other. But don't mistake its silence for simplicity. Non-verbal cues are complex and multifaceted, often expressing emotions or intentions that words may not fully capture.

It's fascinating how non-verbal communication can differ across cultures, yet some fundamental elements—like a smile—seem to be universally understood. Your eyes, for instance, can reveal excitement or boredom, curiosity or indifference. And let's not forget the eloquence of the hands. From a simple thumbs-up to a complex dance of gestures during an animated chat, our hands often talk as much as our mouths do.

Even the space we occupy says something. The distance you keep from someone can indicate intimacy or formality, comfort, or unease. Sometimes, the silence between your words can be just as telling. A prolonged silence might indicate contemplation, awkwardness, or even a shared understanding that needs no words. And let's not overlook the role of touch—a pat on the back, a hug, or even a high-five can speak volumes.

Each of these non-verbal elements contributes to the message we're conveying. If they're in harmony with our spoken words, they enhance understanding and trust. But if they clash, they can create confusion or suspicion. For example, if you say you're fine but your face looks strained, people might doubt your words and wonder what's really going on.

How to Build It

The beautiful thing about skills is that they can be honed, and non-verbal communication is no exception. It's like working on a canvas, each brushstroke improving the overall picture. Let's go through some practical ways to refine this art of silent conversation.

Make Proper Eye Contact

The eyes aren't just the window to the soul; they're a billboard that advertises your attentiveness and sincerity. Establishing solid eye contact shows that you're engaged and interested. However, it's crucial to find a balance; constant staring can be intimidating, while too little can seem dismissive. Start by observing how people respond to your eye contact and adjust accordingly. Aim for meaningful glances that invite connection without overwhelming the other person.

Be Aware of Body Language

Your body can be a powerful spokesperson, speaking volumes without uttering a word. Posture, for example, can indicate confidence or insecurity, openness or defensiveness. The key is self-awareness. Are your arms crossed in a way that might appear defensive? Is your stance inviting or standoffish? Observe others and then bring that same discerning eye to your own body language.

Facial Expressions Don't Lie

There's a wealth of information on your face, whether it's a smirk, a frown, or a wide-eyed look of surprise. Emotions play across our faces like a slideshow, offering clues about our feelings and thoughts. Take note of your facial expressions during different situations. Are you furrowing your brows when confused? Smiling when pleased? Your face tells a story; make sure it's one you want to share.

Play With Your Tone of Voice

Voice can carry an emotional payload just as heavy as any word or phrase. Volume, pitch, and speed all play a part in how our verbal communications are received. If you've ever found yourself saying, "It's not what you said; it's how you said it," you understand the impact tone can have. Experiment with different vocal nuances to discover how they can alter the meaning of your words and affect your interactions.

Pay Attention to Discrepancies in Behavior

We've all met people whose words say one thing, but their non-verbal cues say another. It creates discord that can be off-putting or confusing. The same can happen in reverse; maybe you're saying you're open to feedback, but your crossed arms and stern face suggest otherwise. It's crucial to align your verbal and non-verbal communications for clarity and authenticity.

When in Doubt, Ask

If you find that you're not sure how your non-verbal cues are landing or you're confused by someone else's, there's no shame in seeking clarification. Open dialogue about your observations can dispel misunderstandings and pave the way for more meaningful connections.

Practice Makes Perfect

Just like learning a musical instrument or a new language, improving your non-verbal communication skills will take time and practice. Experiment in different social settings, be it a family gathering or a business meeting. Keep tweaking and adjusting until you find your rhythm.

In essence, your non-verbal cues can either be the harmony that elevates the song of your interactions or the dissonance that confuses your message. Taking the time to improve these skills can lead to richer, more authentic connections with others.

BUILDING RAPPORT AND POSITIVE RELATIONSHIPS

In the realm of emotional intelligence and social skills, rapport goes beyond mere friendship—it's an alignment of emotional energies, a certain synergy of soul. When you're in rapport with someone, there's a mutual understanding, a shared wavelength. You're not just talking; you're connecting.

Building rapport isn't a mere transaction; it's more like growing a garden. You can't force a plant to grow, but you can provide it with the soil, water, and sunlight it needs to flourish. Similarly, rapport blossoms in an environment of mutual respect, shared values, and open communication.

How does one go about nurturing this harmonious relationship? Well, the art of building rapport is part of the "R" in RAIN Selling methodology, which stands for building rapport, asking questions, identifying needs, and establishing the next steps (Schultz, 2019). In essence, if you want to build rapport, it starts with making a genuine human connection, understanding the other person's needs, and valuing the relationship more than the transaction at hand.

So, the next time you find yourself in a social setting, be it a dinner party, a networking event, or just a simple conversation with a stranger, remember that rapport is your golden key to unlocking deeper connections. With a little effort and emotional intelligence, you can turn surface-level interactions into relationships that are rich, rewarding, and mutually beneficial.

How to Build Rapport

So, you've decided to make rapport-building a priority—that's a big win in the realm of social skills. The first step toward building strong relationships is wanting to create them and being intentional about it. Let's dig into the specifics now.

Make a Good Introduction

Before you can begin to build rapport, you've got to break the ice. Your introduction serves as your first impression. So, make it count. It doesn't have to be elaborate; a warm smile, a firm (but not crushing) handshake, and a simple "Hi, I'm [Your Name], nice to meet you" can go a long way.

Actively Listen

Remember, rapport isn't just about talking; it's about listening —really listening. This means not just hearing the words but understanding the emotions and intentions behind them. Active listening is a conscious effort that involves empathy, patience, and sometimes, even biting your tongue. When you show that you're invested in understanding the other person's point of view, you pave the way for a more meaningful connection.

Ask Engaging Questions

Once you've opened the door, keep the conversation going by asking questions that provoke thought and elicit more than a simple "yes" or "no" answer. Open-ended questions like "What brings you here?" or "How do you feel about [topic]?" can offer more room for dialogue and help you learn more about the other person's thoughts and feelings.

Be Aware of Your Body Language

We communicate not just through words, but also through our bodies. So, stand tall, make eye contact, and offer open and inviting gestures. Your non-verbal cues can either reinforce what you're saying or contradict it, so aligning both is crucial to build rapport.

Find Commonalities

Finding common ground can serve as a quick shortcut to rapport. Whether it's a shared interest, a mutual friend, or even a common struggle, these shared experiences can create an instant bond. It's like finding out you both love the same obscure band; it instantly takes the relationship to the next level.

Lead With Empathy and Respect

This is the cornerstone of any strong relationship. If you can put yourself in the other person's shoes and show them respect regardless of the situation, you're well on your way to building rapport that will last.

Building rapport isn't just a one-time effort; it's a continuing process that benefits not just you, but everyone around you. It turns ordinary interactions into memorable ones and acquaintances into genuine friendships. So go ahead, take the plunge, and make building rapport your second nature. You won't regret it.

WRAPPING UP

Just as Dorothy Day reminds us, "We plant seeds that will flower as results in our lives, so best to remove the weeds of anger, avarice, envy and doubt..." Well, my friends, we've been busy gardeners in this chapter, sowing seeds of better social interactions and nurturing the ground for deeper connections.

What we've covered:

- Importance of social skills: We discovered that social skills are not just a "nice-to-have" but essential for better emotional intelligence.
- Effective communication: From verbal exchanges to non-verbal cues, we peeled back the layers of what it really means to communicate well.
- Active listening: We went beyond the usual "nod and smile" to truly understand and empathize with others.
- Building rapport: A deeper dive into forming meaningful relationships by being respectful, showing empathy, and finding common ground.

With each conversation, each meaningful glance, and each genuine interaction, we're cultivating a garden teeming with the flowers of better emotional health, resilience, and yes, even happiness. But let's not get too comfortable just yet; the world of emotional intelligence is vast and filled with possibilities.

In the next chapter, we're going to explore another crucial aspect of emotional intelligence: self-awareness. This is the root system of our garden, nourishing and supporting everything else we've planted.

CASE STUDY: ALAN

Imagine sitting down for coffee with Alan, an IT manager who's aced every technical skill but still feels like something's missing. Alan's got a hunch that his social skills, or lack thereof, are the missing link. So, he decides it's time for a change. This isn't just a story of how Alan climbed the corporate ladder; it's a story of how he became a better listener, a more compassionate friend, and a more intuitive leader.

Alan started where we all should: he got curious about the role of emotional intelligence in social skills. You see, social skills aren't about how many jokes you can tell at a party. They're grounded in emotional intelligence—our ability to read, understand, and respond to emotions in ourselves and others. Alan soon understood that to connect better with people, he had to connect better with himself. It's that soul-deep stuff we often want to dodge but can't afford to.

Now, about communication. Alan thought he was a good communicator, but he came to see that effective communication is a two-way street. You send out a message, and you receive one back; in between is a whole universe of perception, emotion, and interpretation. Alan practiced active listening, a kind of listening where you're not just hearing words but understanding the feelings and intentions behind them.

Alan also discovered the silent but vital role of non-verbal communication. We're talking about the unspoken conversation our bodies are having while our mouths are moving. Our eyes, our facial expressions, and even our posture spill secrets about our true thoughts and feelings. Alan put effort into this quiet dialogue, making sure his body wasn't sending out messages he didn't intend.

Then came the magic of building rapport. Alan was put in charge of a project and decided to apply what he'd learned. He didn't walk into the room as just a manager but as a person genuinely interested in the well-being of his team. He led with empathy, created a space for open communication, and found common ground. His project didn't just meet targets; it soared. And so did Alan. He got a well-deserved promotion and, more importantly, a deeper, more fulfilling connection with those around him.

What Alan learned, and what we've explored here, is that emotional intelligence isn't just a nice-to-have; it's a game-changer. Alan became the hero of his own story, and you can too.

CASE STUDY: JANE

Jane was a pro at her job, navigating spreadsheets and meetings like a champion. Yet, despite her career success, her personal relationships felt superficial. The absence of a deeper emotional connection with her friends, family, and even colleagues was something she couldn't shake off. Then she stumbled upon the idea of emotional intelligence—this intriguing blend of self-awareness and social skills that seemed to be the missing link in her life.

The notion that emotional intelligence is the bedrock upon which social skills are built intrigued her. She started seeing social dynamics in a whole new light. This wasn't about having a vast network of contacts; it was about truly connecting with people, understanding their emotions, and, even more importantly, understanding her own. Emotional intelligence taught her to tune into the emotional nuances in conversations and to navigate interpersonal relationships more sensitively.

But she also learned that effective communication is more than a two-way street—it's a highway built on mutual understanding and respect. She came to see it as an art form. For her, it wasn't just about saying the right things but also ensuring that the other person genuinely understood her and felt understood themselves. This shift in perspective took her interactions from transactional to transformational.

Once she adopted this more nuanced approach to communication, a magical thing happened: her relationships began to flourish. Not just in the 'let's get coffee sometime' sort of way, but genuinely meaningful connections formed. She found it easier to resolve conflicts, not just by finding a solution but by understanding the emotional core of the issue. Empathy wasn't just a word; it was a practice, helping her to step into other people's shoes to feel what they felt. The awareness she developed about her own communication style made her more adaptable, instilling a greater sense of trust among those she interacted with.

Then, there was the discovery of active listening. For Jane, listening had always been a passive activity—something she did in between her turns to speak. She learned the power of truly hearing someone, not just waiting for her chance to reply. This meant maintaining eye contact, reading non-verbal cues like the tilt of a head or the fold of arms, and resisting the urge to interrupt or impose her own solutions. The quality of her conversations skyrocketed, as did the satisfaction she and others got from them.

Of course, the role of non-verbal communication became evident, too. She realized she'd been ignoring a whole channel of human interaction by not focusing on things like eye contact, body language, and even the tone of her voice. A furrowed brow or a dissonant tone could undo even the most well-chosen words. She practiced aligning her body language with her feelings, making her not only more authentic but also easier to understand.

Lastly, she dabbled in the art of rapport. She found that it's one thing to have a conversation and another to have a meaningful connection. Rapport was the secret sauce that turned ordinary interactions into memorable ones. She became a pro at not just talking, but engaging—making a fantastic first impression, keeping conversations alive with great questions, and establishing common ground with just about anyone.

All these little changes started adding up. Jane became the person people could confide in, seek advice from, and genuinely enjoy spending time with. She moved beyond being just competent at her job; she became a true leader—someone who led with emotional wisdom rather than just expertise. But most of all, she found that her relationships, which had always felt like a missing puzzle piece in her life, were now her greatest joy and strength. It was as if she had discovered a hidden layer of life, one that had always been there but she had never seen. And all it took was the willingness to venture beyond her comfort zone and invest in the soft skills that ended up making the biggest difference in her life.

SHARING THE POWER OF
EMOTIONAL INTELLIGENCE

"We cannot tell what may happen to us in the strange medley of life. But we can decide what happens in us — how we can take it, what we do with it — and that is what really counts in the end."

— JOSEPH FORT NEWTON

Emotional hurricanes affect us all at some point in our lives, and until we know how to take charge and hone our emotional intelligence, they can be very difficult to climb out of.

Relationships end... Things happen at work... Disagreements find their way into families and friendship groups... We're ambushed by money worries... Life will always throw challenges our way, and with most of them comes a healthy dose of emotional turbulence.

We'll never be able to stop that from happening, but we can change our reactions, improving our connection with and understanding of others at the same time. As you'll see once you start putting all of this into practice, it's a game-changer, and it becomes much easier to soak up all the joy life has to offer instead of getting bogged down by all the challenges.

Emotional intelligence is a powerful tool, and it can have such a profound impact on your life that I want to help as many people as I can to develop theirs. And this is where I'd like to ask for your help. Don't worry – it won't take long. All I'd like you to do is take a few minutes to spread the word.

By leaving a review of this book on Amazon, you'll direct other people who crave this guidance straight to what they're looking for.

Every review acts as a lighthouse, guiding those who are already searching for the information towards the help they need.

Thank you so much for your support. Life will never stop throwing challenges at us, so it's up to us to take charge.

Scan to leave a review

5

STEP #5—CULTIVATING EMPATHY

> *Emotions are enmeshed in the neural networks of reason.*

— ANTONIO DUMASIO

That quote from neuroscientist Antonio Damasio really resonates—our emotions and reasoning abilities are tied together. How we feel affects how we think. This connection is at the core of what it means to cultivate empathy.

Empathy is about seeing things from another person's perspective, stepping into their shoes, looking through their eyes, and trying to understand their experiences and feelings. Easier said than done, right? We all have our own biases and worldviews that make it challenging to connect on that deeper level.

In this chapter, we'll talk about the common roadblocks to empathy—the tendency to judge quickly, the failure to listen closely, and the lack of curiosity about different viewpoints. However, empathy is a skill we can develop with practice and intention. The rewards make the effort worthwhile.

Imagine how empathy could transform your relationships and daily interactions. Understanding someone's emotions allows you to relate to them in a more genuine way. You build trust and compassion. Conflicts can be resolved by seeking common ground. Even our relationships with ourselves can benefit from self-empathy—understanding rather than criticizing our own feelings and experiences.

I'll share proven techniques to help build your "empathy muscles," making perspective-taking more natural over time. Small mindset shifts that encourage you to listen fully, suspend judgment, and find shared human experiences with those around you. Together, we'll explore this powerful tool for fostering kinder, more caring connections.

WHAT IS EMPATHY?

What is empathy, you ask? It's about connecting to that voice inside all of us that says, "You are seen; you matter." Empathy means opening your spirit to let someone else's light shine in. It's the practice of slipping into their shoes, seeing through their eyes, and walking with them heart-to-heart. When you make space for empathy, you make space for growth, wisdom, and understanding.

Empathy illuminates. When you make the effort to view the world from another's perspective, walls crumble. Conflicts dissolve into mutual understanding. Empathy breeds compassion. It whispers—we are more alike than different, you and I. With empathy as your guide, you move through the world with more patience, more kindness, and more care.

Cultivating empathy elevates your emotional intelligence. Emotional intelligence is the language of the heart—understanding what the heart needs and then speaking its truth with courage and kindness. Empathy fluency is vital. The more empathy flows freely, the wiser our words and actions become. Empathy connects you to your highest self.

At its core, empathy is recognizing the humanity in each of us. It's saying I see you; I feel you; I care. Practicing empathy connects us at a soul level. It lights the path to hope, healing, and a more conscious way of living. When you lead with empathy, you lead with love.

So, nurture your empathy. Let it be a north star guiding you toward deeper self-discovery, richer relationships, and a world united through the power of compassion. When we lead with the heart, we lift humanity. Empathy begets empathy. Spread it generously and watch it multiply.

STEPS TO BECOME MORE EMPATHETIC

The journey to greater empathy starts with curiosity. Make an effort to open your heart to those around you, even strangers or people you perceive as different. Seek to understand their unique stories. When we awaken to each other's inner light with openness, empathy begins to flow more freely.

Focus your awareness on the similarities between yourself and others rather than the differences. Underneath it all, we are more alike than different—we all hope, hurt, and dream. We all desire purpose, belonging, and love. Our shared human experiences far outweigh surface distinctions.

Practice slipping into the shoes of others often. Imagine how their decisions, words, and actions impact those around them from their perspective. When you make the effort to know someone's pain, you become better equipped to offer comfort or support. Walk the path with them in spirit.

Listen deeply and attentively when interacting with others. Offer them your true, uninterrupted presence. Then, share your own experiences vulnerable, too. The door to connection and understanding swings both ways.

Consider joining hands with those marching for justice, equality, and inclusion—causes aimed at lifting up the voices left unheard. In struggle, we evolve. Through service, we transform. Uplifting others uplifts our shared humanity.

Get creative in your quest for empathy. Write stories, draw, play roles, or explore new perspectives through any form of artistry. The heart reveals itself to an open, curious mind. There are infinite paths to walk in another's shoes.

Empathy's river runs deep. Wade into it. Make small efforts to nurture empathy each day. Let it flow freely through you, washing away judgment and misunderstandings. With radical openness, empathy ignites revolution.

OVERCOMING BARRIERS TO EMPATHY

Our fast-paced, disconnected world builds barriers to empathy —but we can dismantle them with patience and intention. Judging too quickly and listening poorly. Fearing differences, these patterns block empathy's flow. When we fail to see each other's humanity, we all suffer.

Slow down, breathe deep. Make time for real connection. Reserve judgment—we all have reasons for our beliefs. Listen fully to understand, not just respond. Seek the shared inner experiences behind surface differences. At our core, we are more alike than different—all deserving of compassion.

Practice gratitude, even for those who challenge you. Thank them for new perspectives. Discomfort opens the mind if you embrace it. Lead with compassion always, even when met with anger. Fighting fire with fire only burns everyone in the end. Stay steady, sharing empathy.

Reflect often on times you felt unheard or misunderstood. Let those memories open your heart to others struggling now. Hurt people inevitably hurt more people. But healed people can choose to heal. Shine light where you found darkness.

Meditate frequently on our interdependence. We need each other now more than ever before. We rise or fall as one people. Empathy is the thread weaving us together into a tapestry of hope. Stay vigilant in mending rips and holes with care.

So, silence the inner critic. Adopt a beginner's mind in every encounter. Make space for empathy to enter. Let it soften hardened edges over time. Stay endlessly curious and endlessly humble. We all have more to learn than we could ever teach.

With empathy's grace, we build bridges. We cease to "other"-ize those unlike us. Inequities are righted, divisions healed. Open hands give and open hearts receive. When I walk in your shoes, you walk in mine. We carry each other's burdens, sharing the load.

REAL-WORLD SCENARIOS FOR PRACTICING EMPATHY

Bridging life's inevitable chasms between us requires opening our hearts to empathy. In the workplace, as in life, opportunities abound to exercise this core human capacity. When we meet each other with radical compassion, even brief interactions can affirm our shared humanity.

The following cases illustrate the power of empathy to heal and connect, even in everyday workplace scenarios. You will read about managers who listened empathetically to struggling team members rather than criticizing from a distance; coworkers who grieved together after a painful loss; and people who found common ground after conflict through vulnerability.

Each example provides a blueprint for weaving more empathy into your daily professional relationships. By suspending judgment, finding commonality, and simply listening with care to colleagues, you, too, can build trust, resolve tensions, and lift others up. With consistent practice, empathy becomes second nature.

The deepest business insights are human insights. These stories reveal that we are not robots checking tasks off a list. We are complex beings seeking purpose and compassion right alongside profitability. When you look past job titles to see the whole human, empathy transforms how you lead, collaborate, and support each other through life's ups and downs.

Sanjay and Alicia

It had been a long, stressful week and tempers were running high on the team. As project manager, I noticed tension brewing between two of my team members, Sanjay and Alicia. They had clashed over project priorities in our last meeting.

I scheduled time to speak privately with each person. With Alicia, I asked how she was feeling about the team dynamic. She confided that she felt dismissed and unheard by Sanjay in meetings. I reflected her feelings back to ensure she felt understood. We discussed her preferred working style and needs.

Next, I met with Sanjay. Rather than criticizing him, I focused on understanding his perspective. He shared feeling overwhelmed and micromanaged lately. I expressed empathy for his situation and asked collaborative questions about what support he needed.

In our 1-on-1s, I simply listened empathetically, resisting the urge to problem-solve immediately. Providing them each a non-judgmental space to share their experiences was powerful. They both felt heard and validated.

At our next team meeting, the mood was far lighter. By leading with empathy, I helped dissolve tension. We determined project priorities together, valuing all voices and ideas equally. My empathy helped their empathy bloom in turn.

Kate

When our team suddenly shifted to remote work during the pandemic, I noticed Kate struggling in our online meetings. She was once lively and outgoing, now quiet and withdrawn. I sensed something deeper was amiss.

Rather than criticizing her disengagement, I decided to have an empathetic conversation. Kate revealed she was feeling extremely isolated, guilty about managing her kids' virtual schooling, and burnt out.

I related to those emotions, sharing my own challenges as a working parent right now. We discussed ways to modify her workload and increase flexibility. I asked how I could better support her needs on our distributed team. Kate felt genuinely heard and cared for.

In our 1-on-1s going forward, I made an effort to check in on Kate's well-being, not just project status. We built-in social time before meetings. I publicly thanked her for her contributions, big and small.

Kate's demeanor improved dramatically. She regained her characteristic zeal and humor. By extending empathy about a difficult situation, I helped Kate feel valued, empowered, and optimistic.

James

When my friend James lost his mom, I could feel the weight of his grief from across the room. I knew that words like "I'm sorry for your loss" wouldn't be enough. Not for this. I also sensed that James needed room to breathe, but how could I reach out without making him feel cornered?

We decided to go for a walk; fresh air has a way of loosening the emotional knots in our chests. So, there we were, the sky stretching out above us as we ventured into the deeper realms of our friendship. I chose to ask him questions about his mom that invited stories rather than yes-or-no answers. What was your favorite thing about her? Do you remember any advice she gave you that sticks out? James's face lit up, and the stories flowed. His eyes sparkled as he shared memories that I could tell were windows into the love he had for her.

He let it slip that in other conversations he'd had, he felt obligated to shelve his grief like some uninvited guest. Hearing this broke my heart. No one should have to closet their grief, especially not for something as inconsequential as workplace etiquette. I told him we could manage without him having to put on a brave face all the time. "We get it, man. Take the time you need. And hey, if it helps, I can take some stuff off your plate for the next little while."

By giving him that space to be unapologetically himself, to feel what he was going through without having to explain or justify it, I hoped to offer a kind of sanctuary. We talked about how to make his life a little easier while he navigated through his grief.

Simple things, like helping with meals and taking walks, so he didn't feel alone.

James thanked me for our walk-and-talk with a sincerity that hit me deep. "You have no idea how much this conversation means to me," he said. In that moment, I realized that empathy isn't just a nice-to-have quality; it's a must-have. We all carry our private struggles, our hidden stories that make us who we are. When we choose empathy, we choose to honor those stories in each other. We go from being people who merely coexist to people who deeply understand and, in that understanding, find a connection that is as humbling as it is profound.

WRAPPING UP

"Emotions are enmeshed in the neural networks of reason." As neuroscientist Antonio Damasio astutely noted, empathy lives at the intersection of heart and mind.

In this chapter, we explored the incredible value of cultivating empathy and practical steps to grow this capacity, including:

- listening deeply without judgment
- taking time to understand different perspectives
- finding common ground and shared experiences
- overcoming biases and barriers through self-reflection
- leading with compassion even when met with anger

By integrating empathy into your daily thoughts and actions, you positively transform relationships and nurture community.

Start small—next time, instead of instant analysis, offer someone your ear. When you stand in their shoes, you just may find you're on the same journey after all.

Now that we've opened our minds to empathy, we'll turn in the next chapter to deepening self-awareness. Knowing ourselves allows us to show up fully for others. Onward in our quest for emotional wisdom!

CASE STUDY: EMILY

Picture this: Emily, a high-flying executive known for her razor-sharp analysis and focus on results. She was top of her game but still felt like something was missing. During a routine check-in, her mentor suggested that what could elevate her leadership even further was cultivating empathy. Emily was initially puzzled. Empathy? Wasn't that just a touchy-feely thing? She decided to dig deeper, realizing that empathy was more than just a warm, fuzzy idea. It was a vital leadership quality that could reshape not only her career but also her life.

The thing about empathy was that it was a complex dance of emotional and cognitive understanding. It was the kind of skill that wove into every aspect of our lives, from our relationships to our work. In a world often drowning in conflict and disconnection, empathy was the lifeboat. Emily began to see that empathy was like the soulmate of emotional intelligence. It wasn't just about understanding your own emotions, but truly feeling and grasping the emotional landscape of others.

With her new knowledge, Emily decided to shake things up at work. She became curious about her colleagues beyond the scope of their professional roles. In meetings, she noticed their body language, heard the hesitations in their voice, and asked questions that invited real, honest answers. Emily realized that focusing on similarities rather than differences brought a team together like nothing else.

She then dove deeper, determined to conquer her own barriers to empathy. She once believed that to be empathetic meant you had to be an open book, which for her felt risky. She learned that empathy wasn't about oversharing but finding a balanced way to listen and be heard, to understand and be understood. It wasn't all rose-tinted; Emily acknowledged that biases and judgments could get in her way. She started practicing mindfulness to help her notice when these barriers were showing up and challenged herself to overcome them.

In a matter of months, Emily witnessed a transformation. Her team was more cohesive, and their productivity had skyrocketed. But more importantly, her relationships—both professional and personal—were richer and more meaningful. Emily became an advocate for social causes she'd previously overlooked, recognizing that empathy didn't stop at the office door; it was a way of being in the world.

So here is the heart of it: When you cultivate empathy, you aren't just becoming a better colleague or a better leader; you become a better human. The landscape of your life transforms, and suddenly, your path seems clearer and more purposeful. It is as if the universe was inviting you to a bigger, richer narrative. That is a pretty powerful outcome.

CASE STUDY: REMIGIO

Remigio, a high school teacher with a no-nonsense reputation, found himself at a crossroads. He was respected, yes, but he was also distant from his students. Despite the high test scores and the disciplined classroom environment, something essential was missing. He sensed that he was failing to connect with his students on a human level. This emotional disconnect was not just in his professional life; it trickled into his personal relationships, too.

Fueled by the unease he felt, Remigio started reading up on emotional intelligence and empathy. At first, he was a bit skeptical. Could these "soft skills" really make a significant difference? Would diving into emotions not make his classroom a mess?

Challenging his own reservations, he started a small experiment. He made it a point to genuinely ask students about their lives, their aspirations, and their worries. No longer was his classroom solely a platform for lectures; it became a stage for shared human experiences.

The transformation didn't happen overnight. Old habits die hard, as they say, and Remigio found himself occasionally slipping back into his old pattern of detached efficiency. But he caught himself, reminding himself that people—whether they are students in a classroom or family at a dinner table—need empathy to thrive.

As weeks turned into months, Remigio noticed a shift in his interactions. He chose to listen deeply when Maria, a usually bubbly student, became withdrawn and silent. Instead of reprimanding her for falling grades, he invited her for a chat. Maria opened up about a turbulent situation at home that was affecting her concentration and self-esteem. Remigio felt like the walls he had built over the years crumbled.

He arranged for Maria to receive emotional support and adjusted her academic workload. Seeing Maria's turnaround was a eureka moment for Remigio, the ultimate validation of his empathic journey. And it didn't stop there. This newfound connectivity made the classroom environment more robust and harmonious, encouraging even the quieter students to engage in discussions and group activities.

The benefits of his transformation rippled into his personal life as well. Conversations with friends and loved ones became more substantial and fulfilling. His ability to navigate emotional undercurrents improved dramatically, leading to stronger, healthier relationships.

So, what's the moral of Remigio's story? Sometimes, the best lessons a teacher can offer are the ones he learns himself. For Remigio, empathy became more than just a teaching tool—it became a way of life, enhancing not only his classroom but also enriching his personal interactions. He realized that the hearts and minds of his students were not compartments but two sides of the same coin, both deserving his attention.

In the end, Remigio learned that being an exceptional teacher meant more than just producing top-grade students; it meant nurturing well-rounded individuals. He wasn't just teaching equations and grammar; he was helping to shape the next generation of emotionally intelligent human beings. And for Remigio, that was the most rewarding lesson of all.

6

STEP #6—MANAGING RELATIONSHIPS

> *Emotions are the glue that holds the cells of the organism together.*

— CANDACE PERT

In this fast-paced world we're living in, it's so easy to lose sight of the things that really matter. And let me tell you, the quality of our relationships is at the top of that list. We're talking about the friendships that lift you up, the love that fills your heart, and even those work connections that make your nine-to-five a bit more bearable. These relationships are our emotional backbone; they keep us standing tall when life tries to pull us down.

So, what's the secret sauce to a relationship that not only lasts but thrives? Well, we're going to dig deep into that. Communication, my friends, is your bread and butter. You've got to talk, listen, and, most importantly, understand each other. Now, don't underestimate the power of emotional intelligence. Recognizing your feelings and the feelings of those around you? That's golden.

But it doesn't stop there. A relationship is a two-way street. Both sides have to want to travel in the same direction. Whether it's your partner, your friend, or your coworker, it's all about working together toward common goals and celebrating each other's wins, big or small.

NURTURING HEALTHY RELATIONSHIPS

Let's talk about something we all yearn for: healthy relationships. Now, what makes a relationship healthy, you ask? First and foremost, it's built on a foundation of trust and honesty. That means no secrets, no shadiness, just pure, open communication. It's a place where both parties feel respected and appreciated, not just as part of a couple but as individuals, too.

When you're in a healthy relationship, both of you should feel secure enough to be your true selves. That's right—no masks, no pretenses. And let's not forget, in a true partnership, both parties share the responsibilities as well as the decisions. It's not a "you or me" situation; it's "us and we."

But here's the kicker: A healthy relationship is one without fear, intimidation, or retaliation. You should never feel like you're walking on eggshells, worried about the repercussions of speaking your truth. Instead, you should feel uplifted, supported, and empowered by your partner.

So, if you're asking yourself, "Is my relationship healthy?" Look for these signs, listen to your inner voice, and most importantly, honor your true self. It's the best gift you can give to yourself and to the relationship. Stay tuned; we're just scratching the surface. Up next, we delve deeper into the magic of maintaining this beautiful bond.

How to Nurture Relationships With Emotional Intelligence

Now that we've talked about what a healthy relationship looks like, let's delve into how to use your emotional intelligence to nurture these connections. You see, emotional intelligence isn't just a buzzword; it's a life skill, a superpower even. It's the key to making your relationships sing.

First things first, keep that communication open, honest, and clear. We all know how easy it is to let misunderstandings brew and fester. Open communication allows you to understand not only what's being said but also the emotional subtext behind it. That's right, it's not just about the words; it's about the feelings and intentions behind those words.

Disagreements are inevitable. But emotional intelligence teaches you to navigate those choppy waters. The goal is not to win an argument but to understand the other person's point of view. It's okay to disagree; it's not okay to dismiss. Address disagreements head-on, but always in a way that maintains both parties' dignity.

You need to create a safe space for emotional connection. In a world that often values tough exteriors, emotional intelligence allows you to be vulnerable and lets others feel safe doing the same with you. When people feel heard and understood, that's when emotional bonds strengthen.

Last but not least, practice empathy. Put yourself in their shoes, feel what they're feeling, and let them know you're right there with them. Not above, not below, just side by side.

So, there you have it. A blueprint for using emotional intelligence to nurture your relationships. Keep these practices in mind, make them part of your daily interactions, and watch how they transform not only your relationships but you as a person. Stick around because we've got more wisdom to share in the next chapter.

CONFLICT RESOLUTION STRATEGIES

Conflicts can be unsettling and disruptive, but often necessary for growth and transformation. So, let's talk about how to navigate through these storms with your relationships intact. Here are ten strategies to tackle conflicts with grace and wisdom.

- **Take a timeout:** We've all been there, getting heated in the moment and wanting to say the first thing that comes to mind. Resist that urge. Stepping away helps you avoid escalation and gives you the opportunity to breathe. During this time, think about what really matters to you in the situation and what you want to accomplish by addressing it. It's a moment of peace before going back to face the storm.

- **Listen, really listen:** It's so easy to interrupt and interject our own thoughts. But hold on a second, literally. When you actively listen, you are giving the other person the space to express themselves fully. This kind of full attention fosters mutual respect and helps you get to the root of the issue. Understanding is the first step toward resolution.

- **Speak your truth, but be kind:** Honesty is the best policy, but delivery is key. Being considerate in your speech doesn't mean watering down your feelings; it means addressing the situation in a respectful manner. Clearly articulate your concerns without blaming or shaming the other person. Your words are powerful; use them to build bridges, not walls.

- **Find common ground:** In any conflict, there's something that you both want—even if it's just a peaceful resolution. Identifying mutual goals can serve as a foundation for constructive dialogue. This shared understanding can help to humanize each party in the eyes of the other, turning opponents into partners working toward a solution.

- **Be open to compromise:** Being rigid in your viewpoints isn't going to get you anywhere. Openness to compromise shows maturity and a willingness to maintain the relationship. Consider alternative solutions that address both parties' concerns. This is a two-way street, and both need to feel satisfied with the outcome.

- **Choose the right time and place:** A calm environment can make all the difference. If tensions are already high, adding a stressful setting to the mix can be a recipe for disaster. Opt for a comfortable location where you can talk openly and freely. Timing and setting are more than just logistics; they set the stage for meaningful dialogue.

- **Stay present:** It's tempting to dredge up the past in a conflict, but this often does more harm than good. Focus on the issue currently on the table and how it can be resolved. Looking back distracts you from the problem at hand, and you risk muddying the waters with unrelated issues. Keep your eyes on the road ahead.

- **Be accountable:** It's not always easy to admit when you're wrong. But doing so is a sign of emotional maturity. Saying sorry can be a powerful gesture that rebuilds trust. It shows you value the relationship more than your ego. Accountability can turn a conflict into an opportunity for growth.

- **Seek third-party help:** Sometimes, the solution is not clear, and an outside perspective can help. A therapist or counselor can offer neutral insights that may reveal the underlying issues. But this isn't a sign of failure; it's a sign of commitment to resolving the conflict and improving the relationship.

- **Agree to disagree:** At times, you'll find that you're at an impasse. Acknowledging that it's okay to have differing opinions can be liberating. This doesn't mean giving up; it means recognizing the uniqueness of each individual. You can respect each other's viewpoints while still maintaining a strong relationship.

So, there you have it! These aren't just strategies; they're life lessons for navigating the complexity of human relationships. Next, we're going to delve even deeper into how to enrich your life through meaningful connections. Stick around; it's going to be enlightening!

BUILDING TRUST AND FOSTERING COLLABORATION

Trust is a word that's packed with so much meaning, isn't it? Imagine for a moment your life without trust. You'd be wading through quicksand uncertain at every turn. Trust is like that invisible thread that weaves the fabric of our relationships, making them strong and resilient. It's not just about having someone's back; it's about knowing they have yours, too. When you trust, you give yourself permission to be your authentic self, and you create space for others to do the same.

Now, I want you to feel this in your core: When you have trust in a relationship, it's like sunshine on a cloudy day. You see, trust lights up the room—or the office, for that matter. It transforms working environments from places of skepticism and doubt to platforms for creativity, cooperation, and collective success. Trust is what makes the difference between a team and a community.

But let's talk about what happens when trust is missing from the equation: the side glances, the whispers, the doubts that eat away at your soul. A relationship without trust is like a car without gas—you're going nowhere fast. And that feeling of uncertainty? That's not just in your head; it's a fog that clouds everyone's judgment and halts progress.

You see, building trust isn't a "one-and-done" kind of deal. It's not a box you can just check off. Trust is a living, breathing entity that needs constant nourishment. Every word you speak, every action you take—they're all brushstrokes in the larger painting of trust. And when you invest in building trust, what you're really doing is investing in a better life for yourself and everyone around you.

HOW TO BUILD TRUST AND COLLABORATION

If you're ready to transform your relationships, your teams, and even your communities, listen up. We're diving into some wisdom here that's not just going to change the game; it's going to change your life. Let's get into it!

First up, let's talk about honesty and direct communication. I'm sure you've heard the saying, "Honesty is the best policy." Well, it's not just a cute phrase; it's the cornerstone of trust. When you're open and transparent, you're not only showing respect to others, but you're also setting the stage for a relationship built on trust. If you say what you mean and mean what you say, you give others permission to do the same. And trust me, that's where the magic happens.

To implement this, begin by setting the tone for open dialogue. Maybe it's a regular team meeting where everyone gets to voice their opinions or concerns. Encourage everyone to be candid but respectful. Show that you value honesty by being the first to communicate openly, and make sure to listen when others follow suit. Trust builds one conversation at a time.

Now, I want you to feel this: Creative collaboration is not just a one-and-done concept—it's a lifeline for innovation. Create spaces and opportunities for your team to brainstorm, dream, and innovate together. Not only will this bring forth fantastic ideas, but it will also help people feel invested in the mission, knowing that their input is valued. Collaborating creatively breaks down barriers and creates a fertile ground for trust to grow.

So, how do we make this real? Start by organizing brainstorming sessions or workshops focused on creative problem-solving. Make sure everyone knows their ideas are welcome, no matter how "out there" they may seem. And let the creative juices flow without judgment—sometimes, the craziest ideas are the seeds for something transformative. Remember, collaboration is a two-way street, so jump in and get your hands dirty, too.

Let's move on to empowering your team to be self-organized. Friends, if you want people to step up, you've got to let them stand up. Give your team the freedom to make decisions, to solve problems, and to truly own their roles. This doesn't mean abandoning structure; it means enabling autonomy within a framework. When people feel empowered, they take on challenges with gusto—and let me tell you, trust thrives in this kind of environment.

Ready to put this into action? It's all about balance. Provide your team with the tools and resources they need, and then step back. Let them take the wheel while you're there as a guide, not as a micromanager. Weekly check-ins can be a great way to stay connected without being overbearing. Trust that they will come to you if they hit a roadblock that they can't navigate around.

Now, here's something that often gets overlooked: clarity in roles and responsibilities. A lot of the time, mistrust comes from misunderstandings and confusion. So do everyone a favor and keep those roles crystal clear. Make sure everybody knows not just what they're doing, but why they're doing it. Clarity reduces friction, and when friction is low, trust can glide right in.

To bring this into your life, take time to clearly outline everyone's roles and responsibilities. Write it down, discuss it, and make sure everyone is on the same page. If possible, involve team members in the process of defining their roles—it leads to greater ownership and understanding. Regularly revisit these roles, especially during times of change, to ensure everyone remains clear on their contributions.

And last but certainly not least, make feedback part of your team culture. Open, constructive feedback is like the water and sunshine for the garden of trust—it helps it grow and flourish. Make it okay to give and receive feedback, both positive and critical. But remember, feedback is not just about pointing out the gaps; it's also about celebrating the wins, big and small.

How do we make this a reality? Create safe spaces for feedback, perhaps through one-on-one meetings or even anonymous suggestion boxes for those who prefer it. Make it a point to ask for feedback during team meetings, showing that it's not only okay but encouraged. And when you give feedback, make it specific, constructive, and immediate. It's not just about what's not working; celebrate the wins, too, and soon enough, a feedback culture will take root.

WRAPPING UP

Let's circle back to our chapter hook by Candace Pert: "Emotions are the glue that holds the cells of the organism together." Just like cells, the members of a team are held together by the glue of trust, emotional intelligence, and effective communication. What we've learned today goes beyond strategy or management lingo; it digs deep into the human elements that can make or break a team's cohesion.

Quick recap:

- Open and honest communication: The cornerstone of trust and collaboration.
- Creative collaboration: A playground for the mind that invites innovation.
- Empowerment: Let your team own their tasks, but provide a safety net.
- Clarity of roles: Keep everyone on the same page to avoid conflicts.
- Feedback culture: A must for growth and continuous improvement.

As we close this chapter, remember that managing relationships isn't just about getting along. It's about nurturing an environment where every team member can thrive, both individually and collectively. So, what's the next vital step on this journey?

Well, let's just say you'll want to stick around because we're about to dig into the power of emotional resilience—your secret weapon for life's most challenging moments. Don't miss it!

CASE STUDY: LUCY

I had this friend in college, Lucy, and the friendship we formed seemed almost serendipitous. We had the same major, ran into each other in three separate classes, and it felt like destiny was practically shouting, "Hey, you two should be friends!" So, we hung out, studied for exams together, and got to know each other's hopes, fears, and, of course, the kinds of food we each swore by during final exam season (mine was pizza; hers was Chinese takeout).

But friendships, much like anything valuable in life, aren't just about the good times. No matter how close you get to someone, there will be moments where you don't see eye-to-eye. For Lucy and me, disagreements came up every now and then. I guess we were both strong-willed and opinionated, which is both a blessing and a curse. There were times when our disagreements seemed like they'd reach a breaking point. Yet we both knew deep down that maintaining our friendship mattered more than winning any argument. So, we made a pact to find healthier ways to deal with conflicts.

One of the most memorable examples was a summer road trip we'd been looking forward to. Now, I was all for soaking in the vibes of small-town diners and sleeping in motels with questionable linens. Lucy, on the other hand, was dreaming of pitching a tent under the stars and hiking up rocky trails. It seemed like we were at an impasse. But instead of canceling the trip or jeopardizing our friendship, we each sat down and made a list of non-negotiables and things we were willing to compromise on. By the end of it, we had a roadmap of cities, campsites, diners, and trails that accommodated both our interests.

Trust is another invisible yet sturdy pillar that held up our friendship. I think we both understood early on that to make our friendship work, we needed more than just shared interests and free weekends. Trust was the currency of our friendship economy, and we built it through unfiltered conversations and being there for each other, no questions asked.

During group projects or planning events together, trust was the undercurrent that made everything run smoothly. We divided tasks based on our strengths, kept each other in the loop, and, most importantly, created a safe space to express our opinions and feedback. And you know what? It was this cycle of trust, collaboration, and open dialogue that not only made our projects successful but also fortified our friendship.

So, if I've learned anything from my years of friendship with Lucy, it's that relationships, whether they are platonic or romantic, are an ongoing project. They need a certain level of emotional finesse. That means being able to navigate conflicts without damaging the relationship, committing to truly understanding the other person, and creating a safety net of trust that catches you both when things get tough.

Take a moment to reflect on your relationships. Are there recurring conflicts that need a different approach? How open and safe is the communication? What steps can you take to foster a greater sense of trust? Because remember, relationships aren't just a key part of life; they are life itself. And understanding how to manage them is a journey well worth the effort.

CASE STUDY: LUCAS

Remember Remigio from the last chapter? Let's see how his mastery of EI impacted his student, Lucas. When Remigio first encountered Lucas, a student in his high school English class, he found himself grappling with frustration and a sense of helplessness. Lucas was known to be disruptive, his actions a loud echo in the hushed hallways of disciplinary action. Other teachers had seemingly written him off, a "troublemaker" stamped invisibly but indelibly on his forehead. Remigio himself had, at first, sighed in resignation, preparing himself for a year of constant disruptions.

But then something changed in Remigio. He began diving deep into the realm of emotional intelligence, learning the nuanced language of empathy, active listening, and effective communication. It was as if someone had handed him a new pair of glasses, bringing the world into sharp, compassionate focus.

Armed with this newfound perspective, he saw Lucas not as a classroom irritant but as a complex individual. He decided to toss the traditional disciplinary playbook and took a radically different approach.

After class one day, Remigio asked Lucas to stay back for a moment. Instead of launching into a lecture, he simply asked, "Hey, you've seemed a bit off lately. Everything okay?" Remigio had prepared himself for a dismissive shrug or a defensive snarl. But Lucas paused. In that silence, the walls of defiance seemed to waver and then crumble. What came out was a torrent of words—Lucas's parents were in the middle of a chaotic divorce, and he felt like he was teetering on the edge of an abyss.

In that moment, Remigio did something he might not have done before his emotional intelligence journey: he listened. Not just passively, but with active, intentional empathy. He didn't interrupt or offer any solutions. He let Lucas speak, only occasionally nodding or offering a quiet "I understand" to encourage him to continue. He also suggested Lucas consider talking to a school counselor, offering to facilitate that connection if it would make things easier.

As weeks turned into months, Lucas began to change. The rowdy interruptions ceased, replaced by tentative, then confident, participation. Remigio noticed that Lucas even started to help others in the class, offering to share his notes or explain a complex point. And as Lucas changed, so did the class dynamic. The students, once wary and distant, started to warm up to Lucas, embracing him as one of their own.

At the end of the school year, Remigio realized the true depth of the transformation. Lucas was not just another student he had "managed" to teach; he was a vivid testament to the life-altering power of emotional intelligence. It was a lesson that

Remigio knew would shape the way he approached teaching—and life—for years to come. It wasn't just about academic achievements or maintaining discipline; it was about reaching into the tangled brush of human emotion and experience and finding a way to nurture the fragile blooms of potential waiting there. And that made all the difference.

7

STEP #7—APPLYING EMOTIONAL INTELLIGENCE PROFESSIONALLY

 As much as 80% of adult 'success' comes from EQ.

— DANIEL GOLEMAN

Now, if that doesn't grab your attention, I don't know what will. We've spent the last six chapters diving deep into the nuances of emotional intelligence and understanding its role in our personal lives. But let's not forget where we spend a massive chunk of our waking hours—our professional lives.

You see, EQ—or emotional intelligence—isn't just a personal affair. It's an office affair, a team affair, and yes, a success affair. This isn't about learning how to "win friends and influence people," although that's certainly a happy byproduct. No, this is about authentic engagement with your work and the people who make that work happen. It's about fostering a better understanding of yourself so that you can navigate the complexities of interpersonal relations in the workplace. It's about realizing your full potential as a leader, a team member, or even as the go-to person when anyone needs advice.

The goal for this final chapter is crystal clear. We're going to explore how mastering emotional intelligence can be a game-changer in your professional life. We're about to bring everything full circle and show you how to make EQ your secret weapon for professional success.

LEVERAGING EMOTIONAL INTELLIGENCE PROFESSIONALLY

You know how we often say that intelligence gets you through the door, but it's your people skills that build the house? Well, that's where EQ comes into play, especially in your career. Remember what Daniel Goleman said? "As much as 80% of adult 'success' comes from EQ." That's huge!

So, you've learned about EQ, but how do you actually put that knowledge to work in your daily grind? First things first, this isn't a once-and-done deal. Your EQ is like your career's emotional pulse—it's always there, always ticking. Think of it as your secret sauce in navigating the maze of office politics and team dynamics.

Going for a promotion or eyeing a leadership role? Your EQ is your ally. When the heat is on and everyone else is losing their cool, you're the one who stays steady. That's the kind of leader people can get behind.

But let's not just focus on the top of the ladder. EQ is just as important in creating meaningful connections with everyone from the mailroom to the boardroom. You're not just "networking"—you're building genuine relationships. This isn't just for the annual office party; it's your lifelong professional circle we're talking about.

What about when things shake up, like a merger or a shift in company strategy? A strong EQ means you can roll with the punches. You're not just surviving these changes; you're the one who's savvy enough to pivot and thrive.

In the end, EQ isn't just a nice-to-have; it's a need-to-have. It's not just about being a team player or a good listener, as important as those are. Your EQ helps you evolve, engage, and excel in your career in a way that sets you apart. So, if you're wondering how EQ fits into the professional picture—trust me, it's not just part of the frame; it's the whole darn painting.

EMOTIONAL INTELLIGENCE IN LEADERSHIP AND TEAMWORK

Do you know how some folks just seem to have that magical touch when it comes to leading a team or collaborating effectively? Chances are, they have a high EQ.

What does EQ mean for leadership and teamwork? For starters, it's the bedrock of effective communication. We're talking about way more than just exchanging pleasantries at the water cooler. Leaders with high EQ have this knack for really "getting" people. They read the room, sense underlying issues, and know when it's time to offer a word of encouragement—or when to back off. The result? A team that feels heard and valued. That's how you create a work environment where people aren't just clocking in and out; they're engaged and committed.

But let's go beyond that. High-EQ leaders aren't just motivators; they're also influencers. Think of the best boss you've ever had. They didn't just bark orders from a corner office, right? They inspired you. They understood what makes you tick and leveraged that to help you reach new heights. It's not about manipulation; it's about cultivating a sense of purpose and belonging. When a leader can create that kind of vibe, productivity isn't just a metric—it's a mission.

And here's another point: EQ is the fuel that keeps the collaborative engine running smoothly. You know how in every group project, there's always that one person who just can't play well with others? With a higher collective EQ, teams are more in sync, better at resolving conflicts, and, frankly, just a lot more fun to be a part of. It's not just about individual contributions; it's about how those contributions come together to create something bigger than the sum of its parts.

In short, a high EQ is important whether you're leading the charge or part of the rank and file. It's the skill that turns group efforts into group successes and maybe—just maybe—makes Monday mornings a bit more bearable.

HANDLING WORKPLACE STRESS AND PRESSURE

We've all been there—Monday rolls around and it feels like the universe has decided to dump a whole load of stress onto your desk. Deadlines are looming, clients are demanding, and let's not even talk about the coffee machine being out of order. This is where the magic of EQ comes into play.

High-EQ individuals are not immune to stress; they just deal with it differently. When you've got a high EQ, you're more in tune with your emotions and how they're affecting your body. Feel that tension creeping into your shoulders? A rapid heartbeat or shallow breathing? Recognizing these physical cues is step one. It's like your body saying, "Hey, something's up. You might want to deal with this."

The next move is to get those emotions out of the driver's seat. It doesn't mean dismissing or suppressing them; it means acknowledging them without letting them dictate your actions. This is easier said than done, of course. However, taking a few deep breaths, stepping away from your desk, or doing some quick mindfulness exercises can serve as emotional circuit breakers, helping you to think more clearly and make more rational decisions.

And here's another tip: leverage the power of empathy. We often think of empathy as something we extend to others, but what about extending it to ourselves? Instead of beating yourself up for feeling stressed, acknowledge that it's okay to feel this way. Self-compassion can actually be a game changer in how you cope with stress.

But let's not forget about your interactions with others. Work is a team sport, and your EQ can make you a better player. If you're sensing tension in the room or picking up on the stress levels of your colleagues, a high EQ allows you to address it in a productive way. Maybe it's offering a word of encouragement, lending a listening ear, or even taking the lead on a group meditation session. After all, a stress-free team is often a more productive one.

In a nutshell, having a high EQ doesn't make workplace challenges go away. But it gives you the tools to tackle them head-on, keeping your cool while you do. And who knows, you might just become the person everyone wants to be around when the going gets tough.

You've come this far, soaking up all this wisdom on EQ and its impact on your career. But let's get down to brass tacks—how do you actually take all this theory and put it into practice? Here are some concrete steps to weave emotional intelligence into your daily professional life.

Practical Steps to Integrate Emotional Intelligence Into Your Professional Life

Step 1: Self-Assessment

The journey starts with you. Take a few minutes every week to reflect on your emotional responses and behavior at work. Did you handle that tense meeting as well as you could have? Were you really present during that client interaction? This isn't about being hard on yourself; it's about understanding where you're at so you can get to where you want to be.

Step 2: Active Listening

We often think we're great listeners, but most of us are just waiting for our turn to speak. The next time you're in a conversation at work, challenge yourself to really focus on the other person. Hear them out completely before formulating your response. You'd be surprised how much this simple change can improve your interpersonal interactions.

Step 3: Empathize, Don't Sympathize

Sympathy is saying, "I'm sorry you're feeling this way." Empathy is putting yourself in their shoes and understanding why they feel that way. The latter is a far more powerful tool in the workplace because it fosters genuine connections.

Step 4: Manage Your Triggers

Identify what sets you off at work. Is it a last-minute deadline? A particular coworker? Knowing your triggers can help you prepare a more emotionally intelligent response. Or, at the very least, give you a few seconds to take those deep breaths we talked about earlier.

Step 5: Seek Feedback

If you want to get better at anything, you've got to be willing to hear how you're doing. Seek out constructive criticism from colleagues and mentors who you respect and admire. And remember, it's not a critique of you as a person—it's an avenue for growth.

Step 6: Foster Team EQ

Believe it or not, emotional intelligence can be contagious. If you're putting all these practices into play, chances are your colleagues will notice and might even get inspired to do the same. Keep an eye out for ways to foster EQ within your team, whether it's through team-building activities, open dialogues about workplace culture, or just being a good role model.

Step 7: Keep Learning

The landscape of emotional intelligence is ever-evolving. Keep up with new studies and articles or even take some online courses to stay on top of your EQ game.

By following these steps, you're not just talking the talk; you're walking the walk. The beautiful thing about emotional intelligence is that it's not a destination but a journey—one that can enrich not just your career but your life as a whole.

So go ahead, roll up those sleeves, and start integrating these steps into your professional life. You've got this.

WRAPPING UP

So, let's circle back to where we started this conversation: "As much as 80% of adult 'success' comes from EQ," Daniel Goleman said. If you've read through this chapter, it's clear that emotional intelligence isn't just a feel-good buzzword; it's the bedrock upon which your career success is built. And if 80% of your success depends on it, then it's worth every ounce of effort you put into it, isn't it?

What you've learned:

- the direct impact of EQ on your career trajectory and why it can't be ignored
- how emotional intelligence benefits leadership skills and team dynamics
- effective ways to manage workplace stress through a higher EQ
- practical steps you can start taking today to weave emotional intelligence into your professional life

Take this knowledge and these tools with you as you go about your daily grind. Recognize your emotional responses, connect genuinely with others, manage your triggers, and most of all, keep growing. Because when you grow emotionally, your professional life will follow suit.

And there it is, the secret sauce to not just surviving in your career, but truly thriving. So go ahead, make Daniel Goleman proud—after all, 80% of your success is calling.

CASE STUDY: ANDRE

Have you ever stopped to wonder why some people just seem to shine at work? I'm not talking about the Ivy League resumes or the hyper-organized project planners. I'm talking about the folks who bring something intangible to the table, who everyone wants on their team. I learned this lesson from my colleague, Andre, whose secret weapon isn't a fancy degree or technical wizardry; it's emotional intelligence.

Let's break it down a bit, shall we? Emotional intelligence isn't just an esoteric concept—it's the quiet pulse of a thriving workplace. Imagine walking into a team meeting where people don't just clock in their opinions like they're punching a time card. Instead, they're fully present, led by Andre, who seems to have an almost sixth sense of the room's emotional temperature. He knows when Sarah is uneasy about a deadline or when Mark isn't speaking up because he feels unheard. By addressing these undercurrents, Andre doesn't just manage a team; he nurtures a community.

We often overlook the "soft skills" like empathy or active listening, dismissing them as less crucial than hard skills. But Andre's career trajectory begs to differ. Every year, like clockwork, he's been climbing that corporate ladder. Not by showing off his spreadsheet skills, although I'm sure they're excellent, but by showcasing something far more important: his humanity.

What's really awe-inspiring is how Andre manages stress. High-stake client meetings, tight deadlines—you name it, he's faced it, and always with remarkable grace. We've all been there, right? The pit in your stomach, the shaky hands. But Andre has a way of transforming that nervous energy into something constructive. He practices deep breathing, he shifts his mindset, but most importantly, he shares these tools with us. The impact on team morale? Immeasurable.

It's not a one-and-done deal for Andre; he's committed to growing his emotional intelligence. He reads, takes courses, and even seeks mentorship. This isn't about navel-gazing; it's about being courageously self-aware. Andre knows his triggers, he understands his boundaries, and he brings this self-knowledge into every interaction.

Skills like coding or finance might get you in the door, but it's emotional intelligence that takes you to the corner office. So, let's pause for some real talk. How emotionally intelligent are you at work? Are you a leader who can sit with discomfort, who can genuinely listen and show up wholeheartedly for your team? And how are you nurturing these qualities in your own professional life?

CASE STUDY: ELLIOT

When Elliot, a rising star at a prestigious marketing firm, was handed the reins of a critical project, everyone expected results as slick and polished as his presentations. But as weeks went by, his team seemed disjointed, their efforts half-hearted. Elliot was baffled; he was an excellent communicator, had top-notch analytical skills, and always aced his performance reviews. So why were things falling apart now?

Around the same time, Elliot stumbled upon a book about emotional intelligence as part of a leadership development course he was taking. Intrigued, he turned to Chapter 7: Applying Emotional Intelligence Professionally. As he read through the concepts of empathetic leadership, effective communication, and the value of emotional self-awareness in the workplace, Elliot had an epiphany.

He began to reassess his leadership style. In meetings, he started focusing on not just the "what" but also the "how." Were his team members engaged? Were they reluctant to voice their opinions? He also realized he had never genuinely asked for feedback; it was always about the deadlines and the deliverables.

Emboldened by his newfound knowledge, Elliot decided to make some changes. He initiated one-on-one check-ins with team members, not to discuss the project, but to understand them better. What were their career goals? What drove them? What were their challenges? The conversations were awkward at first, but as Elliot showed genuine interest, the barriers began to come down.

Taking cues from the chapter, he also implemented active listening in group settings. Gone were the days when he would multitask during team meetings. He paid full attention, encouraged others to speak, and made sure to acknowledge their points before offering his views.

8

EMOTIONAL INTELLIGENCE IN THE DIGITAL AGE

I n our rapidly evolving digital age, the landscape of emotional intelligence (EQ) has experienced a seismic shift. While the core principles of understanding and managing emotions remain steadfast, the avenues for expression, interaction, and interpretation have expanded exponentially. No longer confined to face-to-face encounters or even voice-to-voice telephone calls, our emotional lives have moved into a realm that includes text messages, social media posts, video conferencing, and an ever-growing list of digital platforms. Each of these mediums presents its own unique challenges and opportunities for emotional expression and understanding.

The traditional cues we rely on to gauge someone's emotions—such as facial expressions, tone of voice, and body language—often vanish or become distorted in digital communication. Something as simple as a poorly chosen emoji or an email that seems curt can miscommunicate our intentions or misinterpret someone else's. The risks are not just misunderstandings but also the erosion of emotional connection and the fostering of negativity. However, digital platforms also offer new ways to connect emotionally and understand each other—if we adapt our emotional intelligence skills to this new terrain.

That's why the significance of adapting our EQ skills for virtual interactions cannot be overstated. In a world where remote work is increasingly the norm and friendships can flourish online, understanding how to express empathy, build rapport, and read emotional cues in a digital format is not just useful— it's essential. It's about more than saving face; it's about making sure we're accurately conveying who we are and what we feel in a medium that can easily muddle those messages. Whether you're navigating emotional undercurrents in a work Slack channel or trying to offer genuine support to a friend via text, honing your digital-age EQ skills can make the difference between meaningful connection and frustrating miscommunication.

This chapter will equip you with the insights and tools you need to successfully navigate the complex emotional landscape of today's digital age. From understanding the subtleties of virtual communication to building authentic connections online, we'll explore how to apply and adapt the timeless principles of emotional intelligence in this uncharted territory.

THE DOUBLE-EDGED SWORD OF TECHNOLOGY

Technology is our society's most prominent double-edged sword, particularly when it comes to emotional connections. On the one hand, it's never been easier to reach out, share, and connect with people from all walks of life across every imaginable distance. With a swipe and a click, we can share life updates with hundreds of friends and family members or even create new relationships based on shared interests and goals. But let's not forget the other edge of that sword, where digital interaction can often dilute emotional nuance, leading to misunderstandings or, worse, the breakdown of relationships.

Let's consider the story of Sarah and Maria, two close friends since college. Both women are avid users of social media, but their experiences have been markedly different. Sarah recently moved across the country and has been using video calls and messaging apps to maintain her friendships, including her relationship with Maria. She often shares pictures of her new city, virtually inviting Maria into her life. The technology has facilitated a level of connection that would have been unthinkable in an era of expensive long-distance phone calls and snail mail. In this case, technology acts as a bridge, making a geographically distant friendship feel emotionally close.

Maria, on the other hand, has had a different journey. She uses social media platforms heavily but finds herself feeling increasingly isolated. The "like" and "heart" buttons feel insufficient for expressing her feelings, and she's had her share of disagreements escalate unnecessarily due to the limitations of text-based communication. She misses the days when she could see

Sarah's expressions, hear the tone of her voice, or simply enjoy a moment of silence together without it feeling awkward. For Maria, technology often feels like a barrier rather than a bridge, a constant reminder of the physical and emotional distance that now separates her from her friend.

Then there's Mark, a project manager who has seen the pros and cons of technology play out in the professional realm. Mark manages a remote team and has found tools like Slack invaluable for quick updates and immediate feedback, fostering a sense of team cohesion and collective achievement. Yet, he's also noticed that heavy reliance on digital communication means he's missing out on the emotional cues that naturally occur in a traditional office setting—those off-hand comments before a meeting starts or the subtle facial expressions that indicate confusion, disagreement, or inspiration. Mark finds himself setting up regular video conferences just to "take the pulse" of the team, an extra step that wouldn't be necessary in a physical workspace.

In these stories, the common thread is the need for balance and adaptation. Technology offers incredible tools for emotional connection, but these tools are only as effective as our ability to adapt our emotional intelligence to new forms of communication. The key is not to reject technology but to wield it wisely, understanding its limitations while making the most of its extraordinary capabilities for connection. So, as we continue to text, tweet, post, and video call, let's make sure we're also continuing to listen, understand, and connect—in every sense of those words.

VIRTUAL COMMUNICATION: BEYOND WORDS

In the era of screens and virtual communication, where does emotional nuance fit in? We might not have the luxury of reading facial expressions or interpreting vocal inflections when we're texting or emailing, but that doesn't mean emotional intelligence has no place in digital interactions. It's all about understanding the new cues—tone, timing, and the choice of communication medium—along with a host of digital markers like emojis that are designed to convey emotion.

Let's start with tone. In face-to-face conversations, tone can carry more weight than the words themselves. But when you're typing, how do you convey tone? Punctuation becomes your best friend. Exclamation points can show excitement or urgency; ellipses can indicate hesitation or incomplete thoughts; and a well-placed "haha" can break tension just like a chuckle in person. These tiny markers can help you convey sarcasm, surprise, and everything in between.

Now, what about timing? In digital communication, *when* you say something can be just as important as what you're saying. Sending an urgent email late at night or during the weekend might send the message that you lack boundaries or don't respect the other person's time. On the other hand, timely responses can convey attentiveness and professionalism. In a digital world, where everyone is reachable at all hours, knowing when to reach out matters.

Your choice of communication medium also speaks volumes. In professional settings, an email is often more appropriate than a text, signaling a level of formality and consideration. Among friends, a video call might convey the importance of the conversation you want to have, suggesting it deserves more than a quick text exchange. Being mindful of how your choice of medium sets the tone for the conversation is a crucial part of emotional intelligence in the digital age.

But what about those cute emojis? Far from being frivolous, they've become essential tools for adding emotional context to digital communication. A smiling face can turn a blunt message into a friendly nudge, and a heart can convey warmth and sincerity. Emojis can also cross language barriers, offering a universal method of expressing emotions, approval, or concern. But remember: not all emojis are created equal in all contexts. What works in a text to a friend may not be appropriate in a professional email.

So, while we can't entirely replicate the richness of face-to-face communication in the digital realm, we're far from helpless. By paying attention to these new markers and cues—tone, timing, medium, and even emojis—we can express our emotional intelligence in ways that transcend words. We might be behind screens, but we're still human, after all, and the need for meaningful emotional connection remains a constant.

THE PERILS OF ANONYMITY

Anonymity in the digital age can be both liberating and unsettling. On the one hand, it offers us the freedom to express ourselves without immediate judgment; on the other, it can erode the natural empathetic connections that form through face-to-face interactions. The veil of anonymity can significantly impact emotional intelligence and understanding, often exacerbating miscommunications and enabling less considerate behavior.

The power and immediacy of online communication sometimes make us forget the real human beings on the other end. Take, for instance, the comments section on social media platforms or articles. Discussions can quickly spiral into heated, vitriolic exchanges, with participants showing little regard for the emotional impact of their words. This lack of empathetic connection is often exacerbated by the absence of immediate physical cues like facial expressions and voice tone.

Even in semi-anonymous spaces, such as workplace chat applications, where everyone knows each other but lacks the nuances provided by in-person interaction, misunderstandings can thrive. Without the immediate feedback that comes from facial expressions and vocal tones, messages can easily be misconstrued, creating emotional tension and confusion that can linger.

So, how do we navigate these challenges? Here are some practical tips for maintaining empathy in anonymous or semi-anonymous digital spaces:

- **Pause before you post:** Before hitting "send," take a moment to reread your message. Would you say this to the person's face? If not, you might want to reconsider your words.

- **Humanize the digital:** Remind yourself that behind every username or email address is a real person with feelings and experiences. This perspective can help foster more thoughtful and empathetic interactions.
- **Ask for clarification:** If a message's tone or intent is unclear, don't hesitate to ask for more context. A simple "Could you clarify what you meant by that?" can resolve a lot of misunderstandings.
- **Be explicit about your emotions:** Text-based conversations lack the emotional nuance of face-to-face interactions. If a subject matter is emotionally charged, consider explicitly stating how you feel. For example, "I'm concerned about..." or "That actually makes me really happy."
- **Switch to video or voice:** For important conversations where emotional nuance is crucial, consider switching to a voice or video call. These formats bring back some of the missing context that text alone can't provide.
- **Establish ground rules:** If you're part of a regular online community, whether it's a Slack channel at work or a hobbyist forum, establishing guidelines for respectful interaction can set the tone for more empathetic communication.

By actively employing these strategies, you can help bridge the emotional and empathetic gaps that often accompany digital communication. The aim is not to eliminate the benefits of digital and anonymous interactions but to bring a level of emotional intelligence and understanding that ensures these interactions are as meaningful and respectful as they can be.

SUMMING UP: KEY TAKEAWAYS AND THEIR APPLICATIONS

As we navigate the complex world of digital communication, it's clear that maintaining a high level of emotional intelligence (EQ) is more important than ever. The anonymity or semi-anonymity in online spaces can be a double-edged sword, providing both freedom and potential pitfalls when it comes to empathetic interaction.

Key Takeaways

- **Anonymity affects empathy:** The absence of facial cues and immediate feedback can make it easier to disengage from the emotional reality of interactions, leading to misunderstandings and sometimes, outright hostility.
- **Pause and reflect:** Before posting something online, consider the emotional weight and potential impact of your words. If you wouldn't say it face-to-face, perhaps reconsider.
- **Human element:** Always remember that behind each screen is a real person with their own feelings, beliefs, and experiences.
- **Seek clarification:** If you're unsure about the emotional tone of a digital interaction, don't hesitate to ask for clarification.
- **Be transparent about emotions:** In text-based communication, it's often useful to be explicit about how you're feeling to prevent misunderstandings.

- **Utilize multiple mediums:** For emotionally charged or important discussions, consider switching to voice or video calls to add back the missing layers of emotional nuance.

Applications

The application of these takeaways is not confined to any specific platform or setting. Whether it's a work-related chat application, a social media platform, or an online discussion forum, these principles can be universally applied to improve the quality of digital interactions.

Keep Evolving Your EQ

The landscape of digital communication is continually evolving, and with it, the challenges and opportunities for empathetic interaction also change. As we move further into this digital age, it's crucial to make a conscious effort to continue developing your emotional intelligence skills. Consider this not just a one-off effort, but a journey—one that can bring richer, more meaningful interactions both online and off.

So, keep learning, adapting, and applying these insights. The digital age may offer its set of challenges to emotional understanding, but it also provides a unique platform to practice and improve our empathetic skills. Let's make the most of it.

A CHANCE TO PAY IT FORWARD

As you step forward into the wonderful chapter awaiting you, take a moment to hold the door open for someone else.

Simply by sharing your honest opinion of this book and a little about your own journey, you'll show new readers where they can find all the guidance they need to take control of their future.

YOUR OPINION MATTERS!
LEAVE A REVIEW TO HELP
OTHERS JUST LIKE YOU

Scan to leave a review

Thank you so much for your support. We're all on our own journeys, but every ounce of help we can share makes a huge difference.

CONCLUSION

So, there you have it. We've turned over every stone and explored the hidden corners of emotional intelligence, and hopefully, you've seen just how transformative this thing called EQ can be. It's not just a professional skill; it's a life skill. It's not just about how you manage a team at work; it's about how you manage your relationships, your family, and, yes, even yourself.

Remember the stories we read on this journey? Their successes were not flukes. They invested in their emotional intelligence and turned it into real, tangible change in their professional and personal lives. If they can do it, believe me, so can you. This isn't fiction; it's reality. Your reality. A reality where emotional intelligence is not a footnote but a headline in your life's story.

So, here's my call to action for you: Don't just let these pages gather dust. Make this book a lived experience. Let the lessons marinate, practice them daily, and watch as you become an agent of change—not just in your life but in the lives of those around you. This book is more than just words; it's a catalyst. By incorporating the wisdom here into your own life, you're not just elevating your game; you're elevating the game for everyone around you.

If you've found even a sliver of enlightenment, self-growth, or newfound understanding through this book, don't keep it to yourself. Leaving a review isn't just about praising the book; it's about creating a ripple effect of emotional intelligence. When you share what you've learned, you empower others to discover these truths for themselves. Think of it as passing the torch of enlightenment because when one person rises, we all rise.

I want you to take this as your marching order: Go live your life armed with a nuanced understanding of your emotions and those of others. Go live a life where you're not just surviving, but thriving. Become the architect of your own future, the curator of your relationships, and the CEO of your destiny. The future is not set in stone; it's molded by the choices we make, the people we impact, and the emotional wisdom we wield.

And always, always remember: This is just the beginning, not the finale. The beauty of emotional intelligence is that it grows and deepens with time and practice. Your best is not behind you; it's ahead, waiting for you to seize it. You've got this, and the best is still unfolding. So go ahead and lean into the messy, beautiful, and profoundly human journey of life. Your best chapters are yet to be written, and I can't wait to see where your story goes.

REFERENCES

Are you emotionally intelligent? Here's how to tell. (n.d.). Cornerstone University. https://www.cornerstone.edu/blog-post/are-you-emotionally-intelligent-heres-how-to-tell/

Betz, M. (2022, September 14). *What is self-awareness, and why is it important?* BetterUp. https://www.betterup.com/blog/what-is-self-awareness

Cherry, K. (2023, March 10). *What is self-Awareness?* Verywell Mind. https://www.verywellmind.com/what-is-self-awareness-2795023

Cherry, K. (2023, May 2). *How emotionally intelligent are you?* (n.d.). Verywell Mind. https://www.verywellmind.com/what-is-emotional-intelligence-2795423#:

Day, D. (n.d.). *Emotional intelligence quotes.* Sources of Insight. https://sourcesofinsight.com/emotional-intelligence-quotes/

Dumasio, A. (n.d.). *Emotional intelligence quotes.* Sources of Insight. https://sourcesofinsight.com/emotional-intelligence-quotes/

Emotional intelligence toolkit (n.d.). Helpguide. https://www.helpguide.org/articles/mental-health/emotional-intelligence-toolkit.htm#:

Eurich, T. (2018). *What self-awareness really Is (and how to cultivate it).* Harvard Business Review; hbr.org. https://hbr.org/2018/01/what-self-awareness-really-is-and-how-to-cultivate-it

Fort Newton, J. (n.d.). *Emotional intelligence quotes.* Sources of Insight. https://sourcesofinsight.com/emotional-intelligence-quotes/

Fritz, J., de Graaff, A. M., Caisley, H., van Harmelen, A.-L., & Wilkinson, P. O. (2018). A systematic review of amenable resilience factors that moderate and/or mediate the relationship between childhood adversity and mental health in young people. *Frontiers in Psychiatry, 9.* https://doi.org/10.3389/fpsyt.2018.00230

Goleman, D. (2021). *What is emotional self-awareness?* Kornferry. https://www.kornferry.com/insights/this-week-in-leadership/what-is-emotional-self-awareness

Jenson, E. (n.d.) *Emotional intelligence quotes.* Source of Insight. https://sourcesofinsight.com/emotional-intelligence-quotes/

Mental Health America. (2023). *What is emotional intelligence and how does it apply to the workplace?* Mental Health America. https://mhanational.org/what-emotional-intelligence-and-how-does-it-apply-workplace

Meier, J. D. "Emotional Intelligence Quotes to Help You Master Your Emotions." Last modified August 3, 2013. https://sourcesofinsight.com/emotional-intelligence-quotes/.

Miller, K. (2020, March 13). *Building self-awareness: 16 activities and tools for meaningful change.* PositivePsychology.com. https://positivepsychology.com/building-self-awareness-activities/

Pert, C. (n.d.). *Emotional intelligence quotes.* Sources of Insight. https://sourcesofinsight.com/emotional-intelligence-quotes/

Rosenberg, M. (n.d.). *Emotional intelligence quotes.* Sources of Insight. https://sourcesofinsight.com/emotional-intelligence-quotes/

Schultz, M. (2019, September 18). *How do you build rapport with customers?* RAIN Group Sales Training. https://www.rainsalestraining.com/blog/how-do-you-build-rapport-with-customers#:

Schwantes, M. (2021, June 3). *Here's how to tell within 5 Minutes if someone has high emotional intelligence: skills that anyone can master with practice.* Inc. https://www.inc.com/marcel-schwantes/emotional-intelligence-how-to-tell.html#:

Wallbridge, A. (2023, February 27). *The importance Of self-awareness in emotional intelligence.* TSW Training. https://www.tsw.co.uk/blog/leadership-and-management/self-awareness-in-emotional-intelligence/#:

www.ingramcontent.com/pod-product-compliance
Lightning Source LLC
Chambersburg PA
CBHW030303130626
46549CB00002B/669